COMPOUND
WORDS

COMPOUND WORDS

A quick reference for writers!

by

David R. Christensen

Published by
Press Forward Press
Non-fiction Division
5060 S 710 West
Salt Lake City, UT 84123

Printed in the United States of America
October 2020

Publisher's Information data

Name: Christensen, David R., author/compiler.
Title: Compound words: A quick reference for writers!
Author/compiler: David R. Christensen.
Publisher: Press Forward Press.
Location: Salt Lake City, UT, 84123
Date: October, 2020.
Identifier: ISBN 978-1-940802-27-5

To

Connie A. Walker

What others are saying about
Compound Words

To hyphenate or not to hyphenate, that is the question. Happily, a book has come along to solve that age-old problem. *Compound Words* is the perfect complement to the dictionary and thesaurus for all writers who want to get it right.
--Connie A. Walker, author of
The Wolkarean Inscription* trilogy and *Echoes

Finally, a ready reference of *Compound Words*! Thoughtfully researched, it is quick and simple to use, saving the writer, editor, or communicator from the worst of enemies: doubt.
--Karl Beckstrand, publisher
Premio Publishing & Gozo Books

As a high school Language Arts teacher, I witness the frustration of early writers firsthand. Anything that can simplify that process and help students feel confident is a treasure! Whether for a three-page essay or a full NaNoWriMo submission, *Compound Words* is an excellent quick reference for students and young writers.
--Mary Alexie Baugh
High School Language Arts Teacher

ABOUT THE AUTHOR

In 1973, David R. Christensen graduated from Brigham Young University with a BS degree in civil engineering.

While at college, he developed an interest in writing fiction; sometimes presenting his engineering work in story-form. Sixteen years later, while still working as a consulting engineer, he began a serious study of writing—for children. As a final project for a first correspondence course, he wrote *Tivoli's Christmas*. At the conclusion of a second course, he completed *The Mystery of the Grinning Buddha*. After retiring in 2002, he began polishing off *Tivoli's Christmas*, which was published in November 2008—an illustrated and prize-winning (2005) children's book.

A year later his second book, a mystery for ages 9 to 12, entitled *The Mystery of the Grinning Buddha*, another prize-winner (2006), was published. Two more books in the Millerville Mystery series followed: *The Mystery of the Ugly Bottle* (2010) and *The Mystery of the Haunted Lighthouse* (2013).

David's fifth book was a sci-fi book, entitled **Worlds Without Number** (2014), written for teenagers. And in 2017, David completed a reference book for writers, entitled *Compound Words: A quick reference for everyone!*. This book is a 2020 update, containing about 15,700 words.

WHY THIS BOOK?

The idea for *Compound Words* followed the editing of one of my books. The publisher, and final editor, pointed out several compound words that I got wrong.

Up until then, when I had a question as to whether a compound word was two or more separate words or combined into one word, I searched through one or more of three dictionaries, until I was satisfied I had the word format correct. And there I was with several compound words wrong.

Each of the three dictionaries I referred to above had over 2,000 pages. I relied most heavily on the one most recently published, often comparing its listings with those of the other two as well as with the internet. Sometimes these three dictionaries disagreed with each other as to the best format for a compound word.

For example, my primary dictionary has these two entries: *milk shake* and *after-shave*. The other two dictionaries and the internet all agreed that the best spellings were *milkshake* and *after shave*.

A writer friend of mine once pointed out the first two corollaries of language:

- For every dictionary there is an equal and opposite dictionary.
- Anytime two or more dictionaries agree on anything, a new dictionary will appear and prove why all the others are wrong.

WHAT IS A COMPOUND WORD?

The definition of a compound word that I like best and have found most useful is: *a term made up of two or more words which when combined create a new word with its own unique meaning.*

These new terms might be words combined to make a single word, they might remain separated, or they might be connected with one or more hyphens.

As a side note, none of the dictionaries I used in compiling the body of this book included the term *compound word*, which as defined above, is itself a compound word.

Making things a bit confusing, some compound words may be correct in each of the three forms mentioned above, depending upon how they are used. For example:

- lowrider, low-rider, or low rider;
- terra cotta, terracotta, or terra-cotta;
- hung-over, hung over, or hungover;
- whistleblower, whistle-blower, whistle blower.

ABOUT EXCLUSIONS

Some compound words were intentionally left out of this book because they are either too long to fit on one line of the two-column format used, such as: *chronic obstructive pulmonary disease* or they have use limited to a specialized field, for example: medical, zoological, chemical, athletics, engineering, aeronautics, etc. Fortunately, most of these specialized fields have their own dictionaries.

Compound words belonging to broad groupings, such as plants, animals, astronomy, chemicals, or colors, have, for the most part, also been omitted, for example: *quaking aspen, snail darter, precession of the equinoxes, polytetraflouroethylene, ocean boat blue.*

Also, as a rule, capitalized compound words are not included, for example: African American, San Jose, Pacific Northwest, or Palm Sunday.

Compound words generally considered to be obscene or vulgar are not found in this book, whereas, most slang terms are.

PREFACE

As mentioned above, I have three dictionaries handy at my left elbow. Each has well over 2,000 pages, and I refer to them frequently. Primarily, I use them to make sure I understand the correct usage and spelling of less familiar words. I frequently use these dictionaries to verify the correct form for compound words.

As mentioned earlier, after seeing a list prepared by the editor of one of my books—a list of compound words I got wrong; ones I would have sworn I got right—well, I vowed then and there to compile this book, which contains the vast majority of the most commonly used compound words. In fact, this updated book contains just under 15,700 such entries.

About three years ago, I began the process of examining tens of thousands of dictionary entries for compound words. They are listed alphabetically in this book and in their most common formats: single word, multiple words, or hyphenated words. I also checked the internet for word combinations that have just recently obtained compound-word status. For this updated version, I examined the list of new words for 2017, 2018, and 2019 and included those I felt were relevant.

With that said, I hope you find this update useful.

David R. Christensen
Salt Lake City, Utah

INTRODUCTION

An author is constantly faced with the problem of selecting the correct spelling of words. And, no, the spell checker in his word processor is not foolproof. A grammar checker may reveal a problem when *there* is used in a sentence and *their* should have been, but a person cannot depend on the spell checker to let him or her know all correct or incorrect spellings.

When I first began the research for this book, I had two questions in my mind. First, are there already in existence books similar to the one I would like to have for my own use? Second, are there enough compound words to justify the book I envisioned?

Using Google-search, I found one book written to help the writer deal with compound words. It was written in the 1930s. Its approach was to generate rules a writer could follow to determine whether a word group was compound or not.

Not only did I not want to spend time memorizing a bunch of rules, I had even less interest in memorizing the numerous exceptions that must follow.

Just think how difficult it would be to learn the rules that would explain the following:

- batter bread vs. battercake; bag lady vs. bagman;
- firehouse vs. fire station; hair pick vs. hairpin;
- party animal vs. partygoer; off the grid vs. off-the-wall;

- run-on vs. runout; working girl vs. workingman.

I wanted a book that would help me quickly and easily find a desired entry, enter the correct spelling into my word document, set the book aside, and go on writing.

Now you might wonder if using *this* book is 100% guaranteed to put you in touch with all correct spellings for compound words. I wish it were that easy, but it is not. Language is not an absolute science. It is constantly evolving and changing.

Many years ago, long before I ever wrote my first book report for high school, I discovered I had a fascination with words. I remember taking particular note of the word *cupboard*. Somehow I knew this word, which today is a cabinet mounted on a wall, had its origin as a board attached to a wall and with hooks for holding cups. I concluded then that its original spelling had most likely been: *cup board* and pronounced as two words and not pronounced "cuberd."

Perhaps some two-separate-word words are on their way to becoming single words. Bathroom and bedroom are single words while dining room and living room are still two. We'll have to wait and see.

Interestingly, some two-word compound words will never be combined into one single word. Consider: cross section or cross-section will never become crosssection, since no word in English is allowed to have three of the same letter in succession. The same applies to cross-stitch.

HOW TO USE THIS BOOK

Occasionally the listing of more than one format for a compound word creates an entry too long for a single line on the two-column page layout used in the body of this book. It was therefore important to come up with a method to provide as much information as possible with minimal wording. Note below what is contained within parentheses.

- basketweave, basket weave is listed as: basketweave (basket). The space provided after the first word of the compound word means that a second spelling would be basket weave.
- double-handed, double handed is listed as: double-handed (double). Once again a single space, in this case in place of a hyphen, after the first term denotes two separate words.
- dream catcher, dreamcatcher is noted as: dream catcher (dream). Notice that within the parentheses, there is no space after dream, indicating that the second listing is a single word.
- double knit, double-knit is listed as: double knit (double-) indicating that an alternate spelling is connecting the two words with a hyphen.
- bird watcher, birdwatcher, bird-watcher is listed as: bird watcher (bird) (bird-). Reference to the previous two explanations will make clear the meanings of what is enclosed in parentheses,

namely, a second spelling would be birdwatcher and a third spelling would be bird-watcher.

- give-and-take, give and take is listed as: give-and-take (and). Note the space before and after the word *and* within the parentheses indicates that the second spelling is three separate words.

- gobbledygook, gobbledegook is listed as: gobbledygook (degook) indicating a different way of spelling the last six letters of the listed word.

- musclebound, muscle-bound is listed as: musclebound (muscle-) This indicates that a second spelling is hyphenated.

- pull-down menu, pulldown menu is listed as: pull-down menu (pull) which indicates that the hyphenated portion of the word is sometimes a single word.

At times the first option for a multi-word entry is underlined. This indicates that the first spelling is used more frequently in today's literature. It <u>does not</u> mean that the first spelling is preferred.

And sometimes different spellings apply to different meanings. When this is the case, each word is followed by its part of speech, such as *n.* for noun, *v.* for verb, *adj.* for adjective, etc.

COMMENTS

Not every word in this book is by definition a compound word. Some are phrases made up of more than one word. These are included because a writer might wonder how to spell them as well, for example: *summa cum laude*. Also, some compound words are made up of one actual word and one that is not, for example, *tarradiddle*; some consist of one English word and one foreign word, such as *paper mache*.

A few entries are included just because I like the way they sound, for example, *snollygoster*.

Some compound words are spelled exactly the same and are the same part of speech, yet have totally different meanings. For these, I have added a word after the designation of its part of speech. This makes clear that the spelling is the same for each meaning.

After deciding just which compound words to include in this book, I felt that the most important thing to assure was that the words were spelled correctly and paired accurately.

Although I have intentionally left out most animals, there are exceptions, such as "red herring," which is *a way of preparing herring for consumption* as well as a term meaning *false or misleading clue*.

FINAL WORD

Have you ever considered sitting down and reading a two thousand page dictionary? I admit I had not. But I did. Well, actually I scanned each column of each page of several dictionaries—word by word. One thing I found quite enjoyable, amid this tedium, was making lists of compound words that fit into entertaining and/or amusing categories. See the following examples:

- **Rhyming**: boogie-woogie, fuddy-duddy, house mouse, snail mail, hodgepodge, and more.
- **Changing vowels**: pitter-patter, ticktock, ding dong, wishy-washy, crisscross, and more.
- **Stupid or clumsy**: knucklehead, clodhopper, birdbrain, numskull, half-wit, and more.

Now who said reading a dictionary couldn't be fun?

To view the complete lists mentioned above, check at the end of this book, beginning after page 292.

This and all books by David R. Christensen
are available at
amazon.com

LIST OF WORDS

A

ability grouping

able-bodied

abnormal psychology

A-bomb

abominable snowman

about-face

aboveboard

aboveground

abovementioned

absentee ballot

absentee vote

absent-minded

absent without leave

absolute zero

abstract of title

abuzz

academic freedom

a cappella

access broker

access card

access code

accessory apartment

access road

access time

accident insurance

accident-prone

according as

according to

account executive

acey-deucy

Achilles' heel

acidhead

acid rain

acid reflux

acid rock

acid snow

acid test

acid washing

acquaintance rape

acquired taste

acre-foot

across-the-board

action figure

activated charcoal

active recreation

activewear

act of God

acute care

Adam's apple

add-in

add-on

adhesive tape

ad hoc

ad infinitum

ad interim

Adirondack chair

adjustable-rate mortgage

adjutant general

ad lib *adv*.

ad-lib *v*.

adman

administrative segregation

ad nauseam

ado

ad rem

advanced degree

advanced standing

advance guard

advance man, advanceman

adverse selection

advocacy journalism

adware

aerial ladder

aerosol can

aerospace medicine

affinity card

affinity group

affirmative action

aforementioned

aforesaid

aforethought

aforetime

afoul of

A-frame

Afro-American

Afropop

afterbirth

afterburner

aftercare

afterclap

afterdamp

afterdeck

aftereffect

afterglow

after-hours

afterimage

afterlife

aftermarket

aftermath

afternoon

afterpains

afterripening

afterschool, after-school

aftersensation

after shave (after-)

aftershock
aftertaste
after-tax
afterthought
aftertime
afterword
afterworld
agate line
age group
agency shop
age of consent
age of reason
age-old
age spot
aggravated assault
a gogo, agogo
agony column
ahead of
aidman
airbag
air ball
air base
air bladder
airboat
airborne
air brake
airbrush

airburst
air chamber
air-condition
air-cool
air cover
aircraft
aircraft carrier
aircrew
air cushion
air-cushion vehicle
air dam
airdate
air door
airdrop
air-dry
airfare
airfield
airflow
airfoil
air force
airframe
airfreight
air gun
airhead
air hole
air kiss
air lane

air letter
airlift
airline
airliner
airlock, air lock
airmail
airman
airman basic
airman first class
air marshal
air mass
air mattress
air mile
airmobile
airpark
air piracy
airplane
airplane mode
airplay
air pocket
air police
airport
airpower, air power
air pump
air quotes
air rage
air raid

air rifle
air right
airship
air show
air shower
airsick
air sock
airspace, air space
airspeed
airstrike, air strike
airstrip
air taxi
airtight
airtime
air-to-air
air-to-ground
air-to-surface
air walk
airwaves
airway
airworthy
airy-fairy, airy fairy
AK-47
a la carte
a la king
a la mode
alarm clock

alarm reaction
alehouse
alewife
algor mortis
alienation of affection
A list, A-list
all-American
all around *adv.*
all-around, all-round *adj.*
all clear
all-day
all-embracing
alley cat
alley-oop
alleyway
all-fired
all fours
all get-out, all get out
all hail
alligator clip
all-important
all-inclusive
all-night
all nighter, all-nighter
all-or-none
all-or-nothing
all out *adv.*

all-out *adj.*
all over *adv.*
all-over, allover *adj.*
all-overs
all-powerful
all-purpose
all right
all-star
all-terrain vehicle
all-time
all-wheel drive
alma mater
almshouse
almsman
aloe vera
aloha shirt
alongshore
alongside
alpha and omega
alphanumeric
altar boy
altar call
altar girl
altarpiece
altar rail
altar server
alter ego

alternating current

alternative medicine

alternative school

altitude sickness

ambassador at large

Amber Alert

ambient lighting

ambulance chaser

ambulatory surgery

amen corner

American dream

ammunition clip

amplitude modulation

amusement park

analog computer

anatomically correct

anchor baby

anchorman

anchorperson

anchor store

anchorwoman

ancient history

angel cake

angel dust

angel food cake

angel hair

angle bracket

angle iron

angle of attack

angle of yaw

angle plate

anklebone

annual ring

annular eclipse

answerback

answering machine

answering service

anthill

antianxiety drug

antiballistic missile

antipsychotic drug

anvil cloud

anxiety attack

anxiety disorder

anybody

anyhow

anymore

anyone

anyplace

anything

anytime

Anytown

anyway

anyways

anywhere

anywho, anyhoo

anywise

A-OK, A-Okay

A-one, A-1

apart from

ape-man

applejack

apple pie *n.*

apple-pie *adj.*

apple-polishing

applesauce

April fool

apron string

aptitude test

archangel

archenemy

archway

arc lamp

arc welding

area code

area rug

areaway

arena football

arena theater

argy-bargy

armband

arm candy

armchair

armed forces

armhole

armload

armlock

armor-clad

armored car

armpit

armrest

armstand

arm-twisting

arm wrestling (arm-)

army brat

army group

around-the-clock

arrowhead

art deco, Art Deco

artesian well

art film

art form

art glass

arthouse *adj.*

art house *n.*

article of faith

artificial intelligence

artificial life

art music
art nouveau
art runner
art song
artsy-craftsy
artwork
ashcake
ashcan, ash can
ashtray
aside from
asking price
asphalt jungle
assault and battery
assault gun
assault rifle
assault weapon
assembly line
assemblyman
assemblywoman
assigned risk
assisted living
assisted suicide
asteroid belt
as-told-to
at bat, at-bat
A-team
a tempo

at-home, at home
at-large
atmospheric pressure
atomic age, Atomic Age
atomic bomb
atomic clock
atomic energy
atomic number
atomic pile
atomic reactor
atomic theory
atomic veteran
atom smasher
at-risk
at sign
attaché case
attachment disorder
attackman
attention span
attorney-at-law
attorney general
audiobook
audio card
audiocassette
audio frequency
auld lang syne
aurora australis

aurora borealis
autistic savant
autocross
automaker
automatic pilot
automatic teller machine
automatic writing
autoworker
autumnal equinox
average joe
aversion therapy
aviator glasses
awesome
awestruck
awhile *adv.*
a while *n.*
axman

B

baby back ribs
baby boom
baby boomer
baby buggy
baby bump
baby carriage
babydaddy
babydoll dress

baby grand
babyproof
babysit, baby-sit
babysitter, baby-sitter
baby talk
baby tee
baby tooth
backache
back and forth
backbite
backboard
backbone
backbreaking
back-check
backcountry
backcourt
backdate
back dive
backdoor
backdrop
back-end
backfield
backfill
backfire
backfit
backflip
backflow

background

backhand

backhanded

backhoe

backlash

backlight

backlist

backlit

back-load

backlog

back matter

back nine

back office

backpack

backpedal

backrest

backroom

back seat

back-seat driver

backset

backshore

backside

backslap

backslash

backslide

backspace

backspin

backsplash

backstab

backstage

backstairs

backstay

backstitch

backstop

backstory

backstrap loom

backstretch

backstroke

backswept

backswing

backsword

back talk, backtalk

back-to-back

backtrack

backup

backwash

backwater

backwoods

<u>backyard</u>, back yard

bad blood

bad breath

bad faith

badlands

badmouth, bad-mouth

bad news

bafflegab

bag lady

bagman

bag person

bagpipe

bagwig

bailout

bait and switch

bakeshop

baking powder

baking sheet

baking soda

balance beam

balance sheet

balance wheel

bald eagle

bald-faced

baldhead

balk line, balkline

ball-and-socket joint

ball bearing

ball boy

ball carrier

ball control

ball game, ballgame

ball girl

ball joint

ball of fire

ball of wax

balloon sail

balloon tire

ballot box

ballpark

ball-peen hammer

ballplayer

ballpoint

ballroom

ballroom dance

ball valve

bampot

banana seat

banana split

bandbox

bandleader

bandmaster

band saw

band shell, bandshell

bandsman

bandstand

bandwagon

bandwidth

bandy-legged

bangtail

bang-up
banjo clock
bank account
bank barn
bank bill
bankbook
bankcard
bank discount
bankers' hours
bank holiday
bank machine
banknote
bank rate
bankroll
bank shot
banquet room
banzai attack
baptismal name
baptism of fire
barbed wire
barbell
barbershop
barbwire
barcode, bar code
bareback
bareboat
bare bones

barefaced
barefoot
barefoot doctor
barehanded
bareheaded
bare-knuckle
barelegged
bare-naked
barf bag
barfly
bargain basement
bargaining chip
bargeboard
bargeman
bargirl
bar graph
barhop
barkeeper, barkeep
barmaid
barman
barnburner
barn dance
barn raising
barnstorm
barnyard
barracks bag
barrage balloon

barrel chair

barrelhead

barrelhouse

barrel organ

barrel roll

barrel vault

barrier island

barrier reef

barroom

barstool

bartender

barware

basal reader

baseball

baseboard

baseborn

baseburner

base community

base hit

baseline, base line

baseman

base on balls

base path

base pay

base runner

basic process

basic training

basis point

basketball

basket case

basket catch

basket hilt

basketweave (basket)

basketwork

bass drum

bass fiddle

bass horn

batboy

batgirl

bathhouse

bathing cap

bathing suit

bathmat

bathrobe

bathroom

bath salts

bathtub

bathtub gin

<u>bath water</u>, bathwater

batsman

batter bread

battercake

battering ram

batting average

batting cage
battle-ax, battle-axe
battle cruiser
battle cry
battle fatigue
battlefield
battlefront
battleground
battle group
battle royal
battleship
battleship gray
battlewagon
batwing
bawdyhouse
bay rum
bayside
bay window
beach ball
beach buggy
beach bum
beachcomber
beachfront
beach glass
beachhead
beachscape
beachside

beachwear
beadwork
be all and end all
beanbag
bean ball
bean counter
beanpole
bearbaiting
bearer bond
bear hug
bearskin
beast epic
beast of burden
beat-up
beauty contest
beauty mark
beauty salon
beauty sleep
beauty spot
beauty strip
beaverboard
bed and breakfast
bedbug, bed bug
bedchamber
bed check
bedclothes
bedcover

bedding plant
beddy-bye
bedfast
bedfellow
bed head, bedhead
bed-hop
bedmate
bed molding
bed of roses
bedpan
bedplate
bedpost
bedrock
bedroll
bedroom
bedside
bedside manner
bedsore
bedspread
bedspring
bedtime
bedtime story
bedwarmer
bed wetter
bed-wetting
beefeater
beefsteak

beehive
beekeeper
beeline
beer belly
beer garden
bee-stung
beeswax
beetle-browed
beforehand
beforetime
behindhand
behind-the-scenes
bell-bottom
bell-bottoms
bellboy
bell buoy
bell captain
bell curve
bellhop
bell jar
bell lap
bellman
bell pepper
bells and whistles
bell tower
bellyache
bellyband

bellybutton

belly dance

belly flop

belly-land

belly laugh

belly pack

belly-up

belowground

belt bag

belt highway

belt sander

belt-tightening

beltway

benchmark

bench penalty

bench press *n.*

bench-press *tr.v.*

bench show

bench surgery

benchwarmer

bench warrant

benign neglect

bentwood

besom pocket

best-ball

best boy

best-case

best man

bestseller, best seller

beta test

better half

better-off

betweentimes

bevel gear

bias crime

bias-ply tire

bib and tucker

Bible belt

Bible thumper

bicycle motocross

big band, Big Band

Big Bang

Big Bang theory

big beat

big blind

big-box

big brother, Big Brother

big bucks

big business

big daddy

big data

big deal

big enchilada

Bigfoot

big game	bikini wax
big gun	bilge water
big hair	billboard
big head	billfold
bighearted	billhead
big house	billhook
big kahuna	bill of health
big league *n.*	bill of rights
big-league *adj.*	bill of sale
big lie, Big Lie	billposter
bigmouth	billy club
big-name	billy goat
big science	binary digit
big screen *n.*	binary star
big-screen *adj.*	binge eating
big shot, bigshot	binge-watch
big sister	biological warfare
big stick	biological weapon
big tent	bipolar disorder
big-ticket	birch beer
bigtime, big-time *adj.*	birdbath
big time *n.*	birdbrain
big top	birdcage
big wheel	birdcall
bigwig	bird colonel
bikeway	bird dog *n.*
bikini scar	bird-dog, birddog *v.*

bird feed, birdfeed

bird feeder, birdfeeder

birdhouse

birdman

bird of passage

bird of prey

birdseed

bird's-eye

birdshot

bird watcher (bird) (bird-)

birth control

birth control pill

birthday

birthday suit

birth defect

birth family

birth father

birthing center

birthing room

birthmark

birth mother

birth name, birthname

birth pangs

birth parent

birthplace

birthrate, birth rate

birthright

birthstone

birth weight, birthweight

bishop's cap

biteplate, bite plate

bitewing

bit part

bitstock

bitter end

bitter ender

bittersweet

blabbermouth

black-and-blue

black and white *n.*

black-and-white *adj.*

black art

black bag

black bag job

blackball

black belt

blackboard

black book

black box

black-box warning

black cow

black economy

black eye

blackface

black flag *n.*

black-flag *tr.v.*

black frost

black gold

blackguard

blackhead

black hole

black ice

blackjack

black lead

blackleg

black letter

black light

black liquor

blacklist

black lung

black magic

blackmail

black market *n.*

black-market *tr.v.*

black mass

black money

blackout

black pepper

black powder

Black Power

black sheep

blacksmith

black sufferage

black tea

black tie

blacktop

blackwash

black widow

blah-blah-blah

blameworthy

blanket stitch

blank slate

blast furnace

blastoff, blast-off

blaze orange

bleaching powder

bleary-eyed, blear-eyed

bleeding heart

blended family

blended whiskey

blended wing body

bleu cheese

blind alley

blind date

blindfold

blindman's bluff

blind pool

blindside *tr.v.*

blind side *n.*

blindsight

blind spot

blind tiger

blind trust

blissed-out

blister pack

blitz chess

blitzkrieg

blockade-runner

block and tackle

blockbuster

blockchain

block grant

blockhead

blockhouse

block letter

block party

block plane

block signal

block system

blogroll

blood alcohol level

blood-and-guts

blood bank

<u>bloodbath</u>, blood bath

blood brother

blood clot

blood count

bloodcurdling

blood feud

bloodguilt

blood knot

bloodletting

bloodline

blood money

blood relation

bloodshot

blood sport

bloodstain

bloodstained

bloodsucker

blood sugar

blood test

blood thinner

bloodthirsty

blood type

bloodwork

blotting paper

blow-by-blow

blow-dry

blow dryer

blowgun

blowhard

blowhole

blowout

blowpipe

blowtorch

blowup

blue baby

bluebeard

bluebird day

blue blood, blueblood

blue book, bluebook

blue box

blue cheese

blue chip

bluecoat

blue-collar

blue dog

blue-eyed

blue flu

bluegrass

bluejacket

blue jeans

blue law

blueline, blue line

blue moon

bluenose

blue-pencil

blue-plate

blueprint

blue ribbon

blue-ribbon jury

bluescreen

blue-sky

blue-sky law

blues-rock

blue state

bluestocking

blue streak

Bluetooth

blue water

blush wine

board check

boarder baby

board foot

board game

boarding house

boarding pass

boarding school

boardroom

boardsailing

board shorts, boardshorts

boardwalk

boat hook

boathouse

boatlift

boatload

boatman

boat people

boat shoe

boat train

boatyard

bobbin lace

bobby pin

bobby socks, bobby sox

bobbysoxer

bob skate

bobsled

bobtail

bock beer

bodice ripper

body bag

body blow

bodyboard, body-board

bodybuilder

bodybuilding

body bunker

bodycheck, body check

body clock

body count

body double

bodyguard

body image

body mass index

body mike

body politic

body search

body shield

body shirt

body shop

body slam

body snatcher

body stocking

bodysuit, body suit

bodysurf

bodywork

bogeyman

bogtrotter

bogwood

boilermaker

boilerplate

boiler room

boiling point

boiloff

boldface

bold-faced

bolo knife

bolo tie, bola tic

bolt-action

bolthole

boltrope
bomb bay
bomber jacket
bombproof
bomb rack
bombshell
bombsight
bonbon
bondholder
bondmaid
bondman
bond paper
bondservant
bondsman
bondwoman
bone china
bone conduction
bone-dry
bonehead
bone meal
bonesetter
boneyard
boning knife
bonus issue
boob job
boob tube
booby hatch

booby prize
booby trap
boogeyman, boogieman
boogie-woogie
bookbag
bookbindery
bookbinding
bookcase
book club
bookend
booking office
bookkeeper
bookkeeping
bookmaker
bookmark
bookmobile
bookplate
bookrack
bookseller
bookshelf
bookshop
bookstall
bookstand
bookstore
book value
bookworm
boom box

boomtown

boondocks

boondoggle

booster cable

booster seat

booster shot

boost phase

bootblack

boot camp

bootjack

bootlace

bootleg

bootstrap

bootstrap memory

boozehound

borderland

borderline

borehole

born-again

borrowed time

bossa nova

bottlebrush

bottled gas

bottle episode

bottle-feed

bottleneck

bottom fishing

bottomland

bottom line *n.*

bottom-line *adj.*

bottom round

bottom-up

bouillon cube

boulevard strip

bounty hunter

bow compass

bowel movement

bowfront

bowie knife

bowknot

bowleg

bowlegged

bowline

bowling alley

bowling ball

bowling green

bowman

bow pen

bow saw

bow shock

bowshot

bowstring

bow tie

bow window

bow-wow, bowwow
boxboard
box camera
boxcar
box coat
box cutter
boxer shorts
boxing glove
box kite
box lunch
box magazine
box office
box pleat
box score
box seat
box social
box spring
box stall
box step
box wrench
boyfriend
boy toy
boy wonder
bracket creep
braincase, brain case
brainchild
brain damage

brain-dead
brain death
brain fart
brain freeze
brain-picking
brainpower
brain scan
brainsick
brainstorm
brainstorming
brainteaser
brain trust
brainwash
brainwashing
brain wave
brake drum
brake horsepower
brake light
brake lining
brakeman
brake pad
brake shoe
braking distance
branch water
branding iron
brand name *n.*
brand-name (brand) *adj.*

brand-new
brass band
brassbound
brass-collar
brass hat
brass knuckles
brass ring
brass tacks
brassware
brazenfaced
breach of promise
bread and butter *n.*
bread-and-butter *adj.*
bread and circuses
breadbasket
breadboard
breadbox
breadline, bread line
bread pudding
breadstuff
breadthways
breadwinner
breakaway
breakbeat
break-bulk
break dancing (break)
breakdown

breakeven, break-even
breakfast
breakfront
break-in
breaking and entering
breaking point
breakneck
breakoff
breakout
breakpoint
breakthrough
breakup
breakwater
breast-beating
breastfeed, breast-feed
breastplate
breaststroke
breastwork
breathing room
breathing spell
breathtaking
bred-in-the-bone
breech birth
breechblock
breechcloth
breech delivery
breeches buoy

breechloader

breechloading

breeder reactor

breeding ground

breezeway

brewmaster

brewpub

brick-and-mortar

brickbat

bricklayer

brickwork

brickyard

bridal shower

bridegroom

bride price (wealth)

bridesmaid

bridgeboard

bridgehead

bridge loan

bridgework

bridle path

briefcase

bright-eyed

bright line *n.*

bright-line *adj.*

brightwork

brimstone

bringdown

broad arrow

broadax, broadaxe

broadband

broad-brush

broadcast

broadcloth

broad gauge *n.*

broad-gauge *adj.*

broad jump

broadloom

broad-minded

broadsheet

broadside

broad-spectrum

broadsword

broken-down

broken-field

brokenhearted

broncobuster

Bronx cheer

broodmare

brood patch

broomball

broomstick

brother-in-law

browbeat

brown-bag
brownfield
Brownie point (brownie)
brownnose, brown-nose
brownout
brown patch
brown sauce
brown study
brown sugar
brown water
brunchtime
brushback
brush cut
brushfire, brush fire
brushoff, brush-off
brushstroke
brushwood
brushwork
bubble bath
bubblegum, bubble gum
bubblehead
bubble pack
bubble tea
bubble top
bubble water
bubble wrap
buck-and-wing

buckboard
buck dance
bucket brigade
bucket seat
bucket shop
bucket truck
buck fever
buckhorn
buckjump
buck-naked
buck-passing
buckraking
bucksaw
buckshot
buckskin
bucktooth
buddy-buddy
buddy system
bud vase
buffalo plaid
buffalo robe
buffalo soldier
buffer state
buffer zone
buffing wheel
bugaboo
bugbear

bug dope
bug-eyed
bughouse
bug juice
bug light
bug out
bugged-out
bugle bead
bug-out bag
build-down
building block
build-out, buildout
buildup, build-up
built-in
built-up
bulkhead
bulkie roll, bulky roll
bullbaiting
bullboat
bulldoze
bulldozer
bulletin board
bulletproof
bullet train
bullfight
bullheaded
bullhorn

bullnecked
bullnose
bullpen
bullring
bullroarer
bull rush
bull session
bull's-eye, bull's eye
bull tongue
bullwhip
bully boy
bully pulpit
bullyrag
bumbershoot
bumblebee
bumboat
bumper pool
bumper sticker
bumper-to-bumper
bundt cake
bungee cord
bungee jumping
bunghole
bunk bed
bunker buster
bunkhouse
bunkmate

bunkroom

bunny slope

buntline

burden of proof

burn center

burned-out (burnt-)

burnout

burnsides

burnt offering

burp gun

busboy, bus boy

bushfire

bush jacket

bush league *n.*

bush-league *adj.*

bushman

bushmeat

bush pilot

bushranger

bushwhack

business card

business class

business cycle

business end

businessman

businessperson

businesswoman

busload

busman

busman's holiday

busybody

busy signal

busywork

butcher-block

butcher knife

butcher paper

butler's pantry

butterball

butterfat

butterfingers

butterfly chair

butterfly valve

buttermilk

butterscotch

butthead

butt hinge

butt joint

buttload

button-down

buttonhole

buttonhole stitch

buttonhook

button man

buttonmold

butt pack

butt shaft

buyback

buyer's market (buyers')

buyout

buzz bomb

buzzcut, buzz cut

buzz phrase

buzz saw

buzz term

buzzword

buzzworthy

by and by *adv.*

by-and-by *n.*

by and large

bye-bye

bygone

bylaw

byline, by-line

bypass, by-pass

byproduct, by-product

bystander

byword, by-word

C

cabdriver

cabin boy

cabin class

cabin cruiser

cabinetmaker

cabinetwork

cabin fever

cable box

cable car

cable-laid

cable modem

cable railway

cable-ready

cable-stayed bridge

cable stitch

cableway

cabstand

caesar salad

cafeteria benefit

caffe latte

cakewalk

calendar month

calendar year

calfskin

call-and-response

callback, call back

callboard

call box

call boy

called strike

caller ID

call forwarding

call girl

calling card

call letters

call loan

call number

call-out

call sign

call slip

call to quarters

call-up

call waiting

camelback

camelhair

cameraman

cameraperson

camera-ready

camerawoman

camper shell

campfire

camp follower

campground

camp meeting

camp shirt

campsite

campstool

camshaft

candid camera

candleholder

candlelight

candlelit

candlepin

candlesnuffer

candlestick

candlewick

can-do

candy bar

candy cane

candy-coat

candy corn

candy striper

cane sugar

canker sore

canned goods

canned laughter

cannonball, cannon ball

cannon fodder

canon law

can opener

cant hook

capeskin

cap gun

capital asset
capital gain
capital ship
capital stock
capri pants
cap screw
capstone
captain's chair
captain's mast
carbohydrate loading
car bomb
carbon-14 dating
carbonated water
carbon black
carbon copy
carbon fiber
carbon monoxide
carbon paper
car coat
cardboard
card-carrying
card catalog
cardholder
cardinal point
cardinal virtue
cardsharp
carefree

caregiver
caretaker
careworn
carfare
cargo cult
cargo pants
cargo pocket
carhop
carjack, car-jack
carload
carnal knowledge
carpetbag
carpetbagger
carpet-bomb
carpet sweeper
car phone
carpool, car pool
carriage bolt
carriage trade
carrier pigeon
carrot-and-stick
carrottop
carryall
carrying capacity
carrying charge
carrying-on
carry-on

carry-out

carryover

car seat

carsick

carte blanche

carthorse

cartload

cartop

cartridge belt

cartridge clip

cartwheel

car wash

casebook

case goods

caseharden

case history

case in point

case knife

case law

caseload

casemate

case method

case shot

case study

casework

cash-and-carry

cash bar

cashbook

cash cow

cash crop

cash discount

cash flow

cashier's check

cash machine

cash register

cassette deck

castaway

casting vote

cast iron *n.*

cast-iron *adj.*

castoff

castor oil

casualwear

catalytic converter

cat-and-mouse

catbird seat

catboat

cat burglar

catcall

Catch-22, catch-22

catchall

catch-as-catch-can

catch basin

catchpenny

catch phrase

catchpole, catch poll

catchup *n. ketchup*

catch-up *n. overcome*

catchword

catfight

catgut

cathedral ceiling

catherine wheel

cathouse

catlike

catnap

cat-o'-nine-tails

cat's cradle

cat's eye

cat's-paw, catspaw

catsuit

cattle call

cattle guard

cattleman

cattle prod

catty-cornered (-corner)

catwalk

cauliflower ear

causeway

cave dweller

cave-in

caveman

cayenne pepper

cease-fire, ceasefire

cellblock

cellmate

cell phone, cellphone

cement mixer

center back

center bit

center field

center fielder

centerfold

center forward

centerline

center of gravity

center of mass

centerpiece

center punch

center stage

central bank

central city

centrifugal force

centripetal force

certificate of deposit

certified check

cesspit

cesspool

chafing dish

chainfall

chain gang

chain letter

chainlink fence

chain mail

chain of command

chainsaw, chain saw

chain-smoke

chain store

chairlift

chairman

chairperson

chairwoman

chaise longue

chalkboard

chalk talk

chambermaid

chamber music

chamber of commerce

chamber pot

chamber tomb

change of heart

change of life

changeover

changeup

channel-set

channel-surf

chaos theory

chapbook

chapfallen, chopfallen

chapter and verse

chapter house

character assassination

character dance

character witness

charge account

charge card

charley horse

charm school

charnel house

charterhouse

charter member

charter school

charwoman

chastity belt

chatroom

chattel mortgage

chatterbox

chattering classes

cheapjack

cheap shot

cheapskate

cheat sheet

checkbook

check card

checked swing (check)

checkerboard

checking account

check kiting

checklist

check mark

checkmate

checkoff

checkout

checkpoint

checkroom

cheekbone

cheerleader

cheeseburger

cheesecake

cheesecloth

cheesemonger

cheese-paring

cheesesteak

chef's salad

cherry bomb

cherry-pick

cherry picker (cherry-)

chessboard

chessman

chest of drawers

chest pass

chest register

cheval glass

chewing gum

chicken feed

chicken-fried

chicken-hearted

chicken-livered

chicken scratch

chicken wire

chick flick

chick lit

chief of staff

chief petty officer

childbearing

childbed

childbirth

child-bride

childcare

childfree

child labor

childproof

child's play

chiliburger

chili con carne

chilidog

chili pepper
chili powder
chili sauce
chill factor
chill-out
chill pill
chimneypiece
chimney pot
chimney sweep
chinbone
Chinese checkers
Chinese fire drill
Chinese lantern
Chinese puzzle
chin music
chipboard
chipped beef
chip shot
chitchat
chocolate chip
chocolate-coated
chocolate-covered
chocolate-flavored
chock-full, chockfull
choirboy
choirgirl
choir loft

choirmaster
choke collar
chokehold
chokepoint, choke point
choo-choo
chop block
chop-chop
chophouse
chopping block
chop shop
chopstick
chop suey
chord organ
chorus girl
chowderhead
chowhound
chow line
chow mein
Christmas card
Christmastime
chronicle play
chuck-a-luck
chuckhole
chucklehead
chuck wagon
chugalug
chump change

churchgoer
church key
churchman
churchwarden
churchwoman
churchyard
cinder block
cinder cone
ciphertext
circle graph
circuit board
circuit breaker
circuit court
circuit rider
circular file
circular saw
citizens band
city council
city desk
city editor
city father
city hall
city manager
city room
cityscape
city slicker
city-state

citywide
civic-minded
civil death
civil defense
civil disobedience
civil law
civil liberties
civil marriage
civil rights
civil servant
civil service
civil union
civil war
clack valve
clambake
clam chowder
clam diggers, clamdiggers
clam-flat
clampdown
clams casino
clamshell
clansman
clanswoman
clapboard
clap skate
claptrap
claret cup

clasp knife

class act

class action

class-conscious

classmate

classroom

clawback

claw foot

claw hammer

claw hatchet

claymore mine

clay pigeon

clean and jerk

clean-cut

clean-handed

clean-limbed

clean room

clean-shaven

cleanup

clear-cut

clear-eyed

clearheaded

clearing-house

clear-sighted

cleft lip

cleft palate

clergyman

clergywoman

clerical collar

clickbait

clickstream

clickwrap

client state

cliff dweller

cliffhanger

climate-controlled

climb-down, climbdown

climbing iron

climbing wall

clinch knot

clip art

clipboard

clip joint

clip-on

clipped form

clipsheet

cloak-and-dagger

cloakroom

clock radio

clock-watcher

clockwork

clodhopper

clog dance

cloister vault

close call
close-cropped
closed book
closed-captioned
closed circuit
closed corporation
closed-door
closed-end
closed loop
closed-minded
closedown
closed shop
close-fisted
close-knit
close-mouthed
close-order drill
closeout, close out
close shave
closet drama
close-up
clothbound
clotheshorse
clothesline
clothespin
clothespress, clothes press
clothes tree
cloudburst

cloud chamber
cloud forest
cloudland
cloud nine
cloudscape
cloud seeding
clove hitch
cloven hoof
cloverleaf
club car
club chair
clubface
clubfoot
clubhouse
clubman
clubroom
club sandwich
club soda
club steak
clubwoman
cluster bomb
clutch bag
coach class
coachman
coalfield
coaster brake
coast guard

coastguardsman

coastland

coastline

coast-to-coast

coatdress

coat of arms

coat of mail

coatrack

coatroom

coattail

coatrack, coat rack

coat tree

cobblestone

cock-a-hoop

cock-and-bull story

cockcrow

cocked hat

cockeye

cockeyed

cockfight

cockhorse

cocklebur

cockleshell

cockloft

cockpit

cocktail

cocktail table

cocoa butter

coconut milk

coconut oil

coconut water

code blue

codebook

code name *n.*

code-name *tr.v.*

code red

code word

coffee break

coffeecake

coffeehouse, coffee house

coffeemaker, coffee maker

coffee mill

coffeepot

coffee shop

coffee table

coffee-table book

coffin corner

coffin nail

cog railway

cogwheel

coin-op

coin-operated

cokehead

cold-blooded

cold call
cold cash
cold chisel
coldcock
cold comfort
cold cream
cold cut
cold drink
cold duck
cold-eyed
cold feet
cold fish
cold front
cold-hearted
cold pack
cold shoulder *n.*
cold-shoulder *tr.v.*
cold shower
cold storage
cold sweat
cold turkey
cold war
cold water *n.*
cold-water *adj.*
cold wave
coleslaw, cole slaw
collage film

collarbone
collective farm
collective mark
collective memory
collision course
collywobbles
colorblind, color-blind
colorcast
color-code
colorfast
color-field
color filter
color guard
color line
color wheel
column dress
combat boot
combat fatigue
combat zone
combination lock
comb-over
combustion chamber
comealong, come-along
comeback
comedown
comedy of manners
come-hither

come-on
comfort food
comfort woman
comic book
comic relief
comic strip
coming-out
comity of nations
commander in chief
commanding officer
command module
command post
commercial bank
commercial paper
commercial traveler
commissioned officer
commission merchant
commission plan
commitment ceremony
committeeman
committee of the whole
committeewoman
common carrier
common cold
common ground
common law *n.*
common-law *adj.*

common-law marriage
common market
commonplace
commonplace book
common pleas
common room
common salt
common school
common sense
common stock
common touch
commonwealth
community card
community center
community chest
community college
community property
community service
compact disc (disk)
companion animal
companionate marriage
companionway
company-grade officer
company man
company town
company woman
comparable worth

comparison-shop
compass card
compensatory time
complementary color
complimentary close
composting toilet
compound eye
compound fracture
compound interest
compound microscope
compound word
compressed air
compression fracture
comp time
computer age
computer graphics
computer science
concentration camp
conceptual art
concertgoer
concert grand
concertina wire
concertmaster
concertmistress
concurrent resolution
condensed milk
conditioned response

confectioners' sugar
conference call
confidence game
confidence man
conflict of interest
conga drum
con game
congealed salad
congressman
congressperson
congresswoman
conjoined twin
conjugal rights
conjugal visit
con man
connecting rod
conscience clause
conscience money
conscientious objector
consciousness-raising
consent decree
consignment store
consolation prize
console table
consolidated school
conspicuity tape
conspicuous consumption

conspiracy theory

constitutional monarchy

construction paper

consulate general

consul general

consumer credit

consumer goods

consumer price index

contact flight

contact hitter

contact lens

contact sport

contact tracing

containerboard

containerport

container ship

continental breakfast

continental divide

contingent worker

continuing education

contour line

contour map

control freak

controlled substance

controlling interest

control stick

control tower

convection oven

convenience food

convenience store

conversation piece

converted rice

conveyor belt

cookbook

cookhouse

cookie cutter *n.*

cookie-cutter *adj.*

cookie sheet

cook-off

cookout

cookstove

cooktop

cookware

cooldown

cool-headed

cooling tower

cool jazz

coon's age

coonskin

coping saw

cop-out, copout

copperplate

coppersmith

copperware

copybook

copy boy, copyboy

copycat

copy desk

copyedit, copy-edit

copy girl

copyholder

copyleft

copy protection

copyreader

copyright

copywriter

coral reef

corbel arch

cordless telephone

cordon bleu

cordwood

core inflation

core tool

corkboard

corkscrew

cornball

corn bread, cornbread

corn cake, corncake

corn chip

corncob

corncob pipe

corncrib

corndodger

corn dog

corned beef

cornerback, corner back

corner kick

cornerstone, corner stone

corn-fed

cornfield

corn flakes

cornhusk

cornmeal, corn meal

corn oil

cornrow

corn silk

corn snow

cornstalk, corn stalk

cornstarch

corn sugar

corn syrup

corn whiskey

corporate welfare

corpsman

correspondence course

correspondence school

corrugated iron

cosmetic surgery

cosmic ray
cost-effective
cost of living
cost-of-living adjustment
cost-of-living index
cost-plus
cost-push
costume jewelry
cottage cheese
cottage industry
cotter pin
cotton ball
cotton candy
cotton gin
cotton-picking
cottonseed
cottonseed oil
cotton wool
couch potato
cough drop
cough syrup
councilman
councilwoman
counselor-at-law
countdown
counteract
counterattack

counterbalance
countercheck *n. restrict*
counter check *n. banking*
counterclockwise
counterculture
counterespionage
counterinsurgency
counterintelligence
counterman
countermarch
countermeasure
counteroffer
counterpart
counterplot
counterpoint
counterproductive
counterproposal
counterpunch
counterrevolution
countersign
countersignature
countersink
counterspy
countersue
countersunk
countertop
counterweigh

counterweight

counterwoman

countinghouse (counting)

country and western

country club

country cousin

country-dance

country gentleman

country house

countryman

country mile

country music

country rock

countryside

countrywide

countrywoman

county seat

courseware

courtesy title

courthouse

courtly love

court-martial

court of appeals

court of claims

court of equity

court of inquiry

court of law

court of record

court order

court reporter

courtroom

court tennis

court tomb

courtyard

covenant marriage

coverall

cover boy

cover charge

cover crop

covered bridge

covered wagon

cover girl

cover letter

cover song

cover story

cover-up, coverup

cover version

cowbell

cowboy

cowboy boot

cowboy hat

cowcatcher

cow college

cowgirl

cowhand

cowhide

cowlick

cowman

cowpie

cowpoke

cow pony

cowpuncher

cowshed

cow town

crabmeat

crabstick *n. colored red*

crabstick *n. cudgel*

crack baby

crackbrain

crack cocaine

crackdown

cracked wheat

cracker-barrel

crackerjack

crackhead

crack house

crackleware

crackpot

crackup, crack-up

cradleboard

cradlesong

cradle-to-grave

craft beer

craftsman

craftspeople

craftsperson

craftswoman

craft union

craftwork

cramdown

cramp iron

cram school

crank bait

crankcase

crankpin

crankshaft

crapehanger

crapshoot

crapshooter

crash dive

crash helmet

crash-land

crash landing

crash pad

crash truck

crashworthy

crawlspace, crawl space

crazy bone

crazy quilt
cream cheese
cream of tartar
cream puff, creampuff
cream sauce
cream soda
creature comfort
credibility gap
credit card
credit hour
credit line
credit rating
creditworthy
creepy-crawly
crepe paper
crepe rubber
crew chief
crewcut, crew cut
crewmate
crewmember
crew neck
crew sock
crib death
crisis center
crisscross
critical mass
critical path

crocodile tears
crookback
crop circle
crop-duster, crop duster
crop-eared
cropland
crop rotation
crop top
crossbar
crossbeam
crossbones
crossbow
crosscheck
cross-country
cross-country skiing
crosscourt
cross cousin
cross-cultural
crosscurrent
crosscut
crosscut saw
crosscutting
cross-dress
crossed eyes
cross-examine
cross-eyed
cross-file

crossfire

cross-grained

cross hair, crosshair

crosshatch

crosshead

cross-index

cross-legged

cross matching

cross-national

crossover

crosspatch

crosspiece

cross-pollinate

cross-purpose

cross-question

cross-refer

cross-reference

crossroad

cross section (cross)

cross-selling

cross-step

cross-stitch

crosstalk

crosstie

crosstown, cross-town

cross-train

cross-trainer, cross trainer

cross vault

crosswalk

crossway

crosswind

crossword

crowbar

crowd pleaser

crowdsourcing

crowd surfing

crown colony

crown glass

crown jewel

crown land

crown lens

crown prince

crown princess

crown roast

crown saw

crow's-foot

crow's-nest

crude oil

cruise control

cruise missile

cruiserweight

cruising radius

crybaby

crystal ball

crystal clear (crystal-)
crystal gazing
crystal pleat
crystal radio
crystal set
cubbyhole
cube steak
cubic measure
cubic zirconia
cucking stool
cuckoo clock
cue ball
cue card
cued speech
cufflink, cuff link
culture shock
culture vulture
cupbearer
cupboard
cupcake
cupholder
Cupid's bow
cupid's-dart
curb cut
curb roof
curb service
curbside

curbstone
curb weight
cure-all
curling iron
curl paper
current assets
current income
current ratio
currycomb
curtain call
curtain raiser
curtain speech
curtain wall
curve ball, curveball
custom-built
customhouse
customs bond
customs union
cut-and-dried (-dry)
cut-and-paste
cutaway
cutback
cutdown
cut fastball
cut glass
cutoff, cut-off
cutout

cutover

cutpurse

cut-rate

cutthroat

cutting edge

cutwork

cylinder head

D

dab hand

daddy track

dad joke

daily double

daily dozen

dairy farm

dairymaid

dairyman

dairywoman

daisy chain

daisy cutter

daisy wheel

damage control

dancegoer

dancehall

dance therapy

dancewear

dandy roll

Danish pastry

dark age, Dark Ages

dark comedy

dark horse

dark lantern

darkroom

darning needle

dartboard

dashboard

data bank, databank

database

data processing

data processor

data set

data type

datebook

dateline *n. phrase*

date line *n. International*

dating service

daughter-in-law

dawn patrol

Davy Jones's locker

day bed, daybed

dayboat, day-boat

daybook

daybreak

day camp

daycare, day care

daydream

day job

day labor

day letter

daylight

daylight-saving(s) time

daylong

daymark, day mark

day nursery

day one

daypack

day room

day sailer

day school

day shift, dayshift

days of grace

daystar

day student

daytime

day-to-day

day trade

day trader

day-tripper

daywear

dead air

dead-air space

deadbeat *n. loafer*

deadbeat *adj. indicator*

deadbolt

dead-cat bounce

dead center

dead duck

dead end *n.*

dead-end *adj.*

dead ender

deadeye

deadfall

dead hand

deadhead

dead heat

dead language

dead letter

dead lift

deadlight

deadline

dead load

deadlock

deadly sin

deadman's float

dead march

dead meat

dead-on

deadpan

dead reckoning

dead weight, deadweight

deadwood

deafblind

deaf-mute, deaf mute

dealmaker

dean's list

death angel

deathbed

death benefit

deathblow

death camp

death care

death house

death instinct

death mask

death metal

death penalty

death qualification

death rate

death rattle

death row

death seat

death's-head

deathsman

death squad

death tax

deathtrap

death warrant

deathwatch

death wish

debit card

deck chair

deck hand

deckle edge

deck tennis

decorative art

deejay

deep-dish

deep dive

deep focus

deep freeze *n.*

deep-freeze *tr.v.*

deep freezer

deep-fry

deep fryer

deep pocket

deep-rooted

deep-sea

deep-seated

deep-set

deep six *n.*

deep-six *tr.v.*

deep space

deep-water

deerskin

deerstalker

deeryard

defect-free

defense mechanism

defensive driving

deficit spending

déjà vu

delivery room

delivery system

delta wave

delta wing

demand deposit

demand draft

demand loan

demand note

demolition derby

denatured alcohol

den mother

dental floss

dental hygiene

dental hygienist

dental implant

dental technician

Denver boot

department store

depth charge

depth finder

depth perception

depth sounder

designated driver

designated hitter

desk job

deskman

deskperson

desktop

desktop publishing

dessertspoon

destroyer escort

destroying angel

detail man

detector dog

detention home

devil-may-care

devil's advocate

devil's food cake

dewdrop

dew point

dewy-eyed

dialog box

dial tone

diddly-squat, diddlysquat

die-hard, diehard

die-off

differential gear

digital signature

digital watermark

dilly-dally

dime novel

dime store

diminishing returns

dim-out

dimwit

dine-in

dingbat

ding-dong

dining car

dining room

dinner jacket

dinner theater

dinnertime

dinnerware

diploma mill

dipstick

dipsy-doodle

direct action

direct current

direct deposit

direct examination

direct free kick

direction finder

direct mail

director's chair

director's cut

direct primary

direct tax

dirtbag

dirt bike

dirt-cheap

dirt farmer

dirt-poor

dirty laundry

dirty pool

dirty tricks

dirty word

disabled list

disaster area

disc brake, disk brake

disc jockey, disk jockey

discount broker

discount rate

discretionary account

discretionary income

dish antenna

dishcloth

dishpan

dishpan hands

dishrag
dishtowel
dishware
dishwasher
dishwashing
dishwater
disk drive
disk harrow, disc harrow
disk operating system
disk sander
disk wheel
disorderly conduct
disorderly house
displaced person
distance learning
distance race
distance runner
distress signal
ditty bag
dive-bomb
diving bell
diving board
diving suit
divining rod
dockhand
docking station
dockside

dockworker
dockyard
dodge ball
doe-eyed
doeskin
dog-and-pony show
dog biscuit
dogcart
dogcatcher
dog collar
dog days
dog-ear
dog-eat-dog
dogface
dogfight
doggone
doggy bag, doggie bag
doghouse
dog in the manger
dogleg
dognap
dog officer
do-good
do-gooder
dog paddle
dogpile, dog pile
dog's chance

dogsled, dog sled
dog's life
dog tag
dog-tired
dogtrot
dogwatch
do-it-yourself
do-little
dollar sign
dollar store
dollhouse
dolphin kick
domain name
domestic partner
domestic science
domestic violence
domino effect
domino theory
done deal
donkeywork
donnybrook
donor card
do-nothing
doodly-squat
doo-doo
doofus, dufus
doohickey

doom and gloom
doomsayer
doomsday
doorbell
doorjamb
doorkeeper
doorknob
doorman
doormat
doornail
doorpost
door prize
doorsill
doorstep
doorstop
door-to-door
doorway
doorwoman
dooryard
do-over
doo-wop, doowop
dope sheet
do-rag, doo-rag
dot-com
dot matrix
dotted swiss
double agent

double-barreled

double bass

double boiler

double-book

double-breasted

double check

double chin

double-click

double-cross

double date

double-dealing

double-decker

double digits

double-dip

double-double

double dribble

double-edged

double entry

double-faced

double fault

double feature

double figure

double-handed (double)

double-header (double)

double helix

double-hung window

double indemnity

double jeopardy

double-jointed

double knit (double-)

double negative

double-park

double play

double pneumonia

double-quick

double reed

double reverse

double rhyme

double-space

double standard

double-stop

double take

double talk

double-team

double time

double vision

doublewide

doubting Thomas

doughboy

doughface

doughnut, donut

dovetail

down-and-dirty

down-and-out (and)

61

down-at-heel
downbeat
down-bow, downbow
downburst
downcast
downcourt
downcycle
downdraft
downfall
downfallen
downgrade
downhaul
downhearted
downhill
down-home
downlink
download
down low
downmarket
down payment
downplay
downpour
downrange
downright
downriver
downscale
downshift

downside
downsize
downslide
downslope
downspin
downspout
downstage
downstairs
downstate
downstream
downswing
downtick
downtime
down-to-earth
downtown
downtrend
downtrodden
downturn
down under
downwash
downwind
downzone
draft board
draftsman
draftsperson
draftswoman
drag-and-drop

drag bunt
drag king
draglift
dragline
drag link
dragon lady
drag queen
drag race
drag strip
drainage basin
drainpipe
drama queen
drawback
drawbar
drawbridge
drawdown
drawing board
drawing card
drawing room
drawknife
drawn butter
draw poker
draw shot
drawstring
drawtube
dreadlock
dreadnought

dreamboat
dream catcher (dream)
dreamland
dreamscape
dream team
dreamtime
dream vision
dress circle
dress code
dress-down
dressing-down
dressing gown
dressing room
dressing table
dressmaker
dress rehearsal
dress-up
dresswear
dress weight
drift net
driftwood
drill instructor
drillmaster
drill press
drinking fountain
drip coffee
drip-dry

drip feed

drip pan

dripping pan

dripstone

drive-by

drive-up

driver's seat

<u>drive shaft</u>, driveshaft

drive-through, drive thru

drive time

<u>drivetrain</u>, drive train

drive-up

driveway

droop nose

droolworthy

drop cloth

drop curtain

drop-dead

drop-down menu

drop-in

drop kick

drop leaf

drop letter

droplight

drop-off

dropout

drop pass

dropped egg

drop shot

drop-top

drop zone

drudgework

drug holiday

drug lord

<u>drugstore</u>, drug store

drugstore cowboy

drumbeat

drumbeater

drum brake

drumfire

drumhead

drumhead court-martial

drum machine

drum magazine

drum major

drum majorette

drumroll

drumstick

drunk as a skunk

dryasdust, dry-as-dust

dry cell

dry-clean

dry dock *n.*

dry-dock *tr. & intr.v.*

dry eye
dry farming
dry fly
dry goods
dry hole
dry ice
drying oil
dry kiln
dryland
dryland farming
dry measure
dry mop
dry nurse
dry rot
dry run
dry sink
drysuit
drywall
dry wash
dry well, drywell
dual-purpose
duck blind
duck duck goose
ducking stool
duckpin
ducks and drakes
duck sauce

duck soup
ducktail
duct tape
ductwork
dude ranch
due bill
due date
due process
duffle bag, duffel bag
duffel coat, duffel coat
dugout
dulce de leche
dullsville
dumbbell
dumbfound, dumfound
dumb show
dumbstruck
dumb terminal
dumbwaiter
dumdum *n. bullet*
dum-dum *n. dolt*
dummkopf
dumpsite
dumpster fire
dump truck
dumpy level
dunce cap, dunce's cap

dunderhead	**E**
dune buggy	eager beaver
dunghill	eagle eye
dunk shot	earache
duplex apartment	earbud
dustbin	ear canal
dust bowl	ear candy
dust bunny	eardrop
dust cover	eardrum
dust devil	earflap
dusting powder	earlobe, ear lobe
dust jacket	earlock
dust mite	early bird
dust mop	early music
dustpan	early warning system
dust ruffle	earmark
dust storm	earmuff
dust tail	earned run
dustup	earnest money
Dutch auction	earphone
Dutch courage	earpiece
Dutch door	earplug
Dutch oven	earring
Dutch treat	earshot
Dutch uncle	earsplitting
duty-free	earthborn
dyed-in-the-wool	earthbound, earth-bound

earthenware

earth mother

earthmover

earthquake

earth science

earthshaking

earthshattering

earth station

earthwork

ear trumpet

earwax

earwitness

earworm

easy chair

easygoing, easy-going

easy listening

easy street

eating disorder

eavesdrop

echo chamber

echo check

echo sounder

echo verse

economy of scale

edge city

edge tool

editor-at-large

editor in chief

eeksie-peeksie

efficiency apartment

efficiency expert

effigy mound

egg-and-dart

eggbeater

eggcorn

eggcup

egg drop soup

egghead

eggheaded

eggnog

egg roll

egg timer

ego trip *n.*

ego-trip *intr.v.*

eight ball

eighteen-wheeler

ejection seat

elbow grease

elbowroom

eldercare

electrical storm

electric blanket

electric chair

electric eye

electric light
electron microscope
elementary particle
elephant folio
elevated railway
elevator music
eleventh hour
elliptical galaxy
elliptical trainer
elsewhere
emergency room
emery board
eminent domain
empty-handed
empty-headed
empty nester
empty nest syndrome
enamelware
enamelwork
endangered species
endgame, end game
end leaf
end line
end man
end matter
endnote
endpaper, end paper

endpin
endpoint, end point
end product
end run *n.*
end-run *tr.v.*
end-stage
end-stopped
end table
end use
end user
end zone
energy level
engine block
English horn
English muffin
enlisted man
enlisted woman
enterprise zone
entranceway
entryway
entry word
epic simile
equal opportunity
equal sign
equal temperament
equation of time
erelong

erenow
erewhile
erstwhile
escalator clause
escape artist
escape clause
escape velocity
esprit de corps
essay question
estate tax
ethnic cleansing
ethnic profiling
evaporated milk
evenfall
evenhanded
evening gown
evening star
even keel
even-keeled
even money
evensong
even-steven
even-tempered
event horizon
eventide
event planner
event recorder

everbearing
everblooming
evergreen
evermore
ever-present
everybody
everyday
everyguy
every man jack
everyone
everyplace
everything
everythink
everywhere
evidence bag
evil-disposed
evildoer
evil eye
evil-minded
evil twin
exchange rate
exclamation point
exclusive of
excretion disk
executive agreement
executive function
executive order

executive privilege
executive secretary
executive session
exercise ball
exercise bicycle
exercise book
exhaust pipe
exit door
exit poll
expansion bolt
expansion card
expansion slot
expense account
experiment station
expert system
expiration date
exploded view
exposure meter
express rifle
expressway
extended family
extension cord
extreme unction
eyeball
eyeball-to-eyeball
eye bank
eye bath

eyeblack
eyeblink
eyebolt
eyebrow
eyebrow pencil
eye candy
eye-catching
eye chart
eye contact
eyecup
eye dialect
eye drop
eye drops, eyedrops
eyedropper
eyeglass
eyehole
eyehook
eyelash
eyelid
eyelift
eyeliner
eye opener
eyepiece
eye-popping
eye rhyme
eyeshade
eye shadow

eyeshine
eyeshot
eyesight
eye socket
eyes-only
eyesore
eyestrain
eyetooth
eyewall
eyewash
eyewear
eyewitness

F

face card
facecloth, face cloth
face cord
face-down, face down
face-harden
face-lift, facelift
facemask
face-off
face painting
face-palm, (face , face-)
face plant
faceplate
face-saving

face time
face-to-face
face-up, face up
face value
facial index
fact-finding
fact of life
factory farm
factory ship
fadeaway
face-in, fadein
fade-out, fadeout
fag end
fag hag
fail-safe, failsafe
fail-soft, failsoft
failure to thrive
faint-hearted
fair ball
fair catch
fair copy
fairground
fair-haired
fair market value
fair-minded
fair play
fair shake

fair-spoken
fair trade
fairwater
fairway
fair-weather
fairy godmother
fairyland
fairy ring
fairy tale, fairytale *n.*
fairy-tale *adj.*
fairywand
faith-based
faith healing
fake book
fake news
fallback
fallboard
fall guy
falling action
falling-out
falling rhythm
falling star
falling tide
fall line
falloff
fallout
false alarm

false arrest
false friend
false-hearted
false imprisonment
false memory
false pregnancy
false pretenses
false rib
false start
family jewels
family leave
family man
family medicine
family name
family planning
family room
family style
family tree
family values
family way
fancy dance
fancy dress
fancy-free
fancywork
fangirl
fanjet
fan letter

fanlight
fan mail
fanny pack
fantail
fan vault
faraway
farebeater
fare-thee-well
far-fetched
far-flung
farmer cheese
farmer's lung
farmers' market
farm hand
farmhouse
farmland
farmstead
farmyard
far-off
far-out
far piece
far point
far-reaching
farseeing
far side
farsighted, far-sighted
farthermost

fashionmonger
fashion plate
fastback
fastball
fast break
fast food
fast-forward, fast forward
fast lane
fast one
fast-talk
fast track
fatality rate
fatback
fatberg
fat body
fat cat
fat farm
fathead
father confessor
father figure
father-in-law
fatherland
faultfinder
faultfinding
faux pas
favorite son
fax machine

feather bed

featherbedding

featherboard

featherbone

featherbrain

featheredge

featherstitch

featherweight

federal case

fed up

feeble-minded

feedback

feedback loop

feedbag

feedhorn

feeding frenzy

feedlot

feedstock

feedstuff

fee-for-service

feel-good

fee simple

fee tail

fellow feeling

fellow man, fellowman

fellow servant

fellow traveler

felony murder

fencerow

fence sitter

fender-bender (fender)

Ferris wheel, ferris wheel

ferryboat

fetal position

fever pitch

fever swamp

fiat money

fiberboard

fiberfill

fiberglass

fiber optics

fiberscope

fictitious force

fiddle-de-dee

fiddle-faddle

fiddle-footed

fiddlesticks

fidelity bond

field artillery

field coat

field day

fielder's choice

field event

field glass

field goal

field-grade officer

field guide

field hand

field hockey

field hospital

field house

field jacket

field magnet

field marshal

field officer

field of honor

field of view

field of vision

fieldsman

fieldstone

fieldstrip

field-test

field trial

field trip

fieldwork

fifth wheel

fifty-fifty

fighter-bomber

fighting chair

fighting chance

fighting words

fight-or-flight response

figure eight

figurehead

figure of speech

figure skating

file clerk

filename, file name

file server

fillet mignon

filled gold

filled milk

filling station

fill-up

filmgoer

filmmaker

filmmaking

film noir

filmstrip

filter bed

filter paper

filthy rich

finder's fee

fine art

fine-drawn

fine-grained

fine print

fine-spun

fine-tooth comb
fine-tune
fingerboard
finger bowl
fingerbreadth
finger hole
fingernail
finger-paint
finger painting
fingerpick
finger point *n.*
finger-point *v.*
finger-pointing
finger post
fingerprint
finger puppet
fingerspelling
finger stick, fingerstick
finger-stool
fingertip
finger wave
finishing school
finishing touch
finish line
fipple flute
fire alarm
fire and brimstone

firearm
fireback
fireball
firebase
fireboard
fireboat
firebomb
firebox
firebrand
firebreak
fire-breathing
firebrick
fire brigade
firebug
<u>fire clay</u>, fireclay
fire control
firecracker
fire-damaged
firedog
fire door
firedrake
fire drill
fire-eater
fire engine
fire escape
fire extinguisher
firefight

firefighter, fire fighter
fireflood
fireguard
firehose
firehouse
fire hydrant
fire irons
firelight
firelock
fireman
fire marshal
fire opal
firepit
fireplace
fireplug
firepower
fireproof
fire-resistant
fire retardant
fire sale
fire screen
firesetter
fire ship
fireside
fire station
firestone
firestorm

fire tower
firetrap
fire truck
firewall
firewater
firewood
firework
firing line
firing pin
firing squad
firmware
first aid
first base
first baseman
firstborn
first class *n.*
first-class *adj.*
first cousin
first-degree burn
first down
first edition
first family
first finger
first floor
first fruits, firstfruits
first-generation
first gentleman

firsthand	fish farm
first-in, first-out	fish flour
first lady	fishgig
first lieutenant	fishhook
first-line	fishing expedition
first mate	fishing rod
first name	fish ladder
first night	fishmeal
first offender	fishmonger
first person	fishnet
first quarter moon	fishplate
first-rate	fishpond
first responder	fish stick
first run	fish story
first sergeant	fishtail
first strike	fishwife
first string	fission bomb
first-timer	fist bump
first water	fistfight
fiscal year	five-and-ten
fish and chips	five hole
<u>fishbowl</u>, fish bowl	five-spice powder
fish cake	fixed annuity
fisherman	fixed income
fisherman's bend	fixed oil
fisherman's knot	fixed-point
fisherwoman	fixed star

fixed wing
fixer-upper
flag carrier
flag football
flagman
flag of convenience
flag officer
flag of truce
flagpole
flagship
flagstaff
flagstick
flag-waving
flake tool
flak jacket
flameout
flameproof
flame retardant
flamethrower
flankerback
flannel cake
flapdoodle, flap-doodle
flareback
flare-up
flashback
flashboard
flashbulb, flash bulb

flash burn
flash card, flashcard
flashcube
flash drive
flash flood, flashflood
flash-forward
flash-freeze
flashgun
flash lamp
flashlight
flash memory
flash mob
flashover
flash point, flashpoint
flash tube
flash unit
flatbed
flatbed press
flatboat
flatbottom
flatbread
flatcar
flatfoot
flat-hat
flatiron
flat iron (flatiron) steak
flatland

flatline

flat out *adv.*

flat-out *adj.*

flat panel *n.*

flat-panel *adj.*

flat pick

flat race

flat screen *n.*

flat-screen *adj.*

flat silver

flat tax

flattop

flatware

flat-water

flatwork

flavor of the month

fleabag

fleabite

flea-bitten

flea collar

flea-flicker

flea market

flesh and blood

fleshpot

flesh wound

fleshy fruit

flex-fuel

flextime

flibbertigibbet

fiftyfold

flight attendant

flight bag

flight crew

flight deck

flight engineer

flight feather

flight jacket

flight line, flightline

flight path

flight plan

flight recorder

flight surgeon

flight-test

flightworthy

flimflam

flint glass

flintlock

flipbook

flip chart

flip-flop

flip side

flip turn

floating dock

floating-point

floating rib
floatplane
floodgate
floodlight
floodplain, flood plain
flood tide
floodwall
floodwater
floodway
floorboard
floorcloth
floor exercise
floor lamp
floor leader
floor-length
floor manager
floor plan
floor sample
floor show
floorwalker
flophouse
floppy disk
flotation device
flow chart, flowchart
flower bud
flower child
flower girl

flower people
flowerpot
flow meter
flow sheet
flowstone
flubdub
flue pipe
flue stop
fluidextract
fluid mechanics
fluid ounce
flutter kick
flux gate
fly ash
flyaway
fly ball
fly book
flyboy, fly-boy
flyby, fly-by
fly-by-night
fly-cast
fly front
fly gallery
flying boat
flying bomb
flying bridge
flying buttress

flying field

flying head

flying jib

flying machine

flying mare

flying saucer

flying squad

flying start

flying wedge

flying wing

flyleaf

fly net

flyover

flypaper

flypast

fly rod

flysheet

flyspeck

fly swat

fly swatter

flytrap

fly-tying

flyway

flyweight

flywheel

flywhisk

foam board, foamboard

foam core, foamcore

foam rubber

focal length (distance)

focal point

focus group

foeman

fog bank

fogbound

fogbow

fogdog

foghorn

foldaway

foldboat

folding money

foldout

foldup

folk art

folk dance, folkdance

folk magic

folk Mass, folk mass

folk medicine

folk music

folk-rock, folk rock

folksinger, folk singer

folk song, folksong

folktale, folk tale

folkway

follow-on	foot-and-mouth disease
follow shot	footbag
follow-through (through)	football
follow-up, followup	footbath
food bank	footboard
food chain	footboy
food court	footbridge
food fish	foot-candle
food insecure	foot-dragging
food insecurity	footfall
foo dog	foot fault
food pantry	footframe
food poisoning	footgear
food processor	foothill
food pyramid	foothold
food service	footlights
food stamp	footlocker
foodstuff	footlong
food stylist	footloose
food web	footman
foolhardy	footmark
foolproof	footnote
fool's cap	footpace
fool's errand	footpad *n. thief*
fool's gold	footpad *n. foot*
fool's paradise	footpath
foosball	footprint

footrace, foot race

footrest

footrope

foot rot

footslog

foot soldier

footsore

footstall

footstep

footstone

footstool

footwall

footway

footwear

footwork

forasmuch as

forbidden fruit

forced march

force-feed

force field

force-march

forcemeat

force of habit

force-out

force play

force pump

force quit

fore and aft *adv.*

fore-and-aft *adj.*

fore-and-after

fore-and-aft rig

fore-and-aft sail

foreign affairs

foreign aid

foreign-born

foreign correspondent

foreign exchange

foreign legion

foreign policy

forensic medicine

forestland

forest ranger

forget-me-not

forgotten man

for-instance

forkball

forklift

forlorn hope

formalwear

formfitting

form letter

formwork

forthcoming

forthright

forthwith

fortnight

fortune cookie

fortune hunter

fortuneteller

forty-five

forty-niner

forty winks

forward contract

forward dive

forward-looking

forward pass

fossil fuel

foul ball

foul line

foulmouthed

foul play

foul shot

foul tip

foul-up

found art

found object

found poem

fountainhead

fountain pen

four-bagger

four-by-four

four-cycle

four-dimensional

four-eyed

four eyes

four flush *n.*

four-flush *intr.v.*

four-footed

fourhanded

four-in-hand

four-leaf clover

four-letter word

four-poster

fourscore

foursome

foursquare

fourth dimension

fourth estate

fourth wall

four-way

four-wheel drive

four-wheeler

fowling piece

foxhole

foxtrot *intr.v.*

fox trot *n.*

fraidy cat

frame of reference

frame story

frame-up

framework

Frankenfood

Franklin stove

frankpledge

freak flag

freak-out, freakout

freak wave

free agent

free alongside ship

free-associate

free association

freeboard

freeboot

freebooter

freeborn

free city

freediving, free-diving

freedman

freedom fighter

freedom of speech

freedom of the seas

freedom rider

freedwoman

free enterprise

free fall, freefall

free-fire zone

free-floating

free-for-all

freeform

freehand *adj.*

free hand *n.*

freehanded

freehearted

freehold

free kick

free-living

freeload

free love

free lunch

freeman

free market

freemason

freemasonry

free on board

free port

free-range

free rein

free ride

free riding, freeriding

free safety

free silver

free skating

free sledding
free soil *n.*
free-soil *adj.*
free speech
free spirit
free-spoken
freestanding
freestyle
free-swimming
free-swinging
freethinker
free thought
free throw
free throw lane
free-throw line
free trade
free university
free verse
freeware
freeway
free weight
freewheel
freewill *adj.*
free will *n.*
free world
freewriting
freeze-dry

freeze-etching
freeze-frame (freeze)
freezer burn
freezing point
free zone
freight car
freight train
French braid
French bread
French chalk
French chop
French cuff
French curve
French door
French dressing
french fry, French fry *n.*
french-fry *tr.v.*
French harp
French heel
French horn
French-inhale
French kiss
French knot
French leave
Frenchman
French pastry
French press

French provincial

French seam

French toast

French window

Frenchwoman

frequency illusion

frequent flyer (flier)

fresh breeze

freshwater

fretboard

fret saw, fretsaw

fretwork

Freudian slip

friction drive

friction match

friction tape

fried dough

Friendsgiving

friendly fire

fright wig

fringe benefit

fringing reef

frock coat

frog kick

frogman

frogmarch

frontage road

front bench

frontcourt

front-end

front-end load

front-end loader

frontiersman

frontierswoman

frontline

frontlist

front-load

frontman

front matter

front money

front nine

front office

front-page

front room

front-runner, frontrunner

frontside

front-wheel drive

front yard

frostbite

frost-free

frost heave (boil)

frost line

frostwork

fruit beer

fruitcake

fruit cocktail

fruit sugar

frying pan

fuddy-duddy

fudge factor

fuel cell

fuel-efficient

fuel injection

fuel oil

fuel rod

fullback

full blood

full-blooded

full-blown

full-bodied

full-bore

full circle

full-court press

full disclosure

full dress *n.*

full-dress *adj.*

fuller's earth

full-fashioned

full-fat

full-fledged

full gainer

full house

full-length

full load

full marks

full metal jacket *n.*

full-metal-jacket *adj.*

full monty

full moon

full-mouthed

full nelson

full rhyme

full ride

full-scale

full-service

full-size

full spread

full stop

full-throttle

full-time

fully-automatic

fully-equipped

fully fashioned

functional illiterate

function key

function word

funded debt

funeral director

funeral home

fun fair

fun house, funhouse

funk hole

funnel cloud

funny bone

funny book

funny farm

funnyman

funny money

funny paper

funnywoman

furthermore

furthermost

fused sentence

fusible metal

fusion bomb

fusion voting

fussbudget, fuss-budget

fusspot

future perfect

future shock

future tense

futurity race

futurity stakes

fuzzyheaded

fuzzy logic

G

gabfest

gadabout

gaff-topsail

gag law

gag line

gagman

gag order

gag rule

gal Friday

gallbladder, gall bladder

galley slave

gallop rhythm

gallows humor

gallstone

gambrel roof

gamekeeper

game law

game of chance

game plan

game point

game room

game show

game warden

gangbuster

gangland

gangplank

gang plow
gang saw
gangway
gap-toothed
gap year
garage sale
garbage collector
garden apartment
garden hose
garment bag
garrison cap
garter belt
gasbag
gas bladder
gas burner
gas chamber
gas fitter
gas giant
gas-guzzler
gasholder
gashouse
gaslight
gaslit
gas log
gas main
gas mask
gas station

gastight
gas turbine
gasworks
gatecrasher
gated community
gatefold
gatehouse
gatekeeper
gate-leg table
gatepost
gateway
Gatling gun
gavel-to-gavel
gearbox
gearhead
gear ratio
gear shift
gear train
gearwheel, gear wheel
geek chic
gee whiz *interj.*
gee-whiz *adj.*
gee-whizzery`
gee willikers
Geiger counter
gemstone
gender bender (gender-)

gender-fluid
gender gap
gender-neutral
genderqueer
gene pool
general admission
general anesthesia
general anesthetic
general assembly
general aviation
general court-martial
general delivery
general election
general officer
general partnership
general practitioner
general-purpose
general relativity
general staff
general store
generating station
generation gap
genetic code
genetic engineering
Geneva gown
gentle breeze
gentlefolk

gentleman
gentleman-at-arms
gentleman farmer
gentleman's agreement
gentleman's gentleman
gentlepeople
gentleperson
gentlewoman
geodetic survey
geologic time
geomagnetic pole
geomagnetic storm
geometric progression
geometric series
German measles
German silver
germfree
germ theory
germ warfare
getaway
get-go
get-together
get-tough
getup
get-up-and-go
get-well
ghetto blaster

ghost dance

ghost pepper

ghost story

ghost town

ghost word

ghostwrite

ghostwriter

giant slalom

giant star

giddyup, giddyap, giddap

gift card

gift certificate

gift of gab

gift of tongues

gift-wrap

gig economy

gillnet *tr.v.*

gill net *n.*

gillnetter

gill slit

gilt-edged

gimlet-eyed

gimme cap

ginger ale

ginger beer

gingerbread

gingersnap

gin mill

gin rummy

girl Friday

girlfriend

girl wonder

give-and-take (and)

giveaway

giveback

given name

glacial valley

glad hand *n.*

glad-hand *v.*

glad rags

glamourpuss, glamorpuss

glam rock

glass blowing (glass)

glass ceiling

glassed-in

glass eye

glasshouse

glass jaw

glassmaker

glassware

glass wool

glasswork

glee club

gleeman

glen plaid

glide path

global brightening

global dimming

global warming

globetrot

globular cluster

gloom and doom

glory hole

glottal stop

glove box, glovebox

glove compartment

glow plug

glycemic index

go-ahead

goal-driven

goal fest

goalkeeper

goal kick

goal line

goalmouth

goalpost, goal post

goalside

goaltender

goaltending

go-around

goatskin

go bag

gobbledygook (degook)

go-between

go-by

go-cart

go cup

God-awful

godchild

goddaughter

go-devil

godfather

godforsaken (God)

godhead

godhood

godmother

godparent

God's acre

godsend

godson

Godspeed

go-getter

goggle-eyed

go-go *adj. dance*

go-go *adj. assertive*

going-over

goings-on

goldbeating

goldbrick *n. shirker*

gold brick *n. guilded*

gold coast

gold digger

golden age

golden ager

golden calf

golden goal

golden handcuffs

golden handshake

golden oldie

golden parachute

golden rule

golden section

golden syrup

goldfield

gold-filled

gold fix, gold fixing

gold foil

Goldilocks zone

gold leaf

gold mine

gold rush

goldsmith

gold standard

golf ball

golf club

golf course

gondola car

good afternoon

Good Book

goodbye, good-bye

good day

good evening

good faith

good-fellowship

good-for-nothing

goodhearted

good-humored

good-looking

goodman

good morning

good nature

good-natured

good night

good offices

good old (ol', ole) boy

good-sized

good-tempered

good turn

goodwife

goodwill, good will

goody bag

goody-goody

goody two-shoes
goofball
goof-off
goofproof
goo-goo
goose bumps (goose)
goose egg
goose flesh
gooseneck
gooseneck hitch
gooseneck trailer
goose pimples
goose step *n.*
goose-step *intr.v.*
gopher ball
go-round
gospel music
Gospel side
gossipmonger
governor-general
gownsman
grab bag
grace cup
grace note
grace period
grade crossing
grade point

grade point average
grade school
grad school
graduate school
graham cracker
graham flour
grain alcohol
grain elevator
grain sorghum
gram equivalent
grammar school
grandaunt
grandbaby
grandchild
granddad
granddaddy, grandaddy
granddaughter
grand duchess
grand duchy
grand duke
grande dame
grandfather
grandfather clock
grandfather paradox
grand jury
grandkid
grand larceny

grandma

grand march

grand master, grandmaster

grandmother

grandnephew

grandniece

grand opera

grandpa

grandparent

grand piano

grand slam

grandson

grandstand

grand tour

granduncle

grand unified theory

graniteware

granny flat

granny knot

granny woman

grant-in-aid

grantsmanship

grapefruit

grapeshot

grape sugar

grapevine

graphic arts

graphic design

graphic equalizer

graphic novel

graphics processor

graph paper

grass cloth

grasshopper

grassland

grassroots

grasstops

grass trimmer

grass widow

grass widower

grave accent

gravedigger

graven image

grave robber

graveside

gravestone

graveyard

graveyard shift

graving dock

gravitational force

gravity assist

gravy goat

gravy train

gray area

graybeard

gray literature

graymail

gray market

gray matter

grayshirt

graywater

greaseball

grease gun

grease monkey

greasepaint, grease paint

grease pencil

greasy spoon

great-aunt, great aunt

great circle

greatcoat

great divide

greathearted

great room

great seal

Great Spirit

great-uncle, great uncle

greenback

greenbelt

green card

green-eyed

green-eyed monster

greenfield

greengrocer

greenhorn

greenhouse

greenhouse effect

greenhouse gas

green light *n.*

greenlight (green-) *tr.v.*

greenlit

greenmail

greenmarket

greenroom

greensand

greenscreen

greens fee

greenside

greenskeeper

green soap

greenstrip

green tea

greenware

greenwashing

greenway

greeting card

Gregorian chant

griddlecake

gridiron

gridlock
grillroom
grillwork
Grim Reaper
grind rail
grindstone
gripsack
gristmill
groomsman
gross anatomy
gross-out
ground ball, groundball
ground bass
groundbreaking
ground cloth
ground cover
ground crew
ground fault
ground floor
ground glass
groundkeeper
ground loop
groundout
ground plan
ground rule
ground rule double
ground sheet

groundside
groundsill
groundskeeper
ground speed, (ground)
ground state
ground stroke
groundswell
groundwater, (ground)
groundwork
ground zero
group home
group insurance
group practice
group therapy
groupthink
groupware
growing pains
grow light
grownup, grown-up n.
grown-up adj.
growth factor
growth hormone
growth ring
grubstake
G-string
G-suit
guardhouse

Guardmember

guard of honor

guardrail

guardroom

guardsman

guesstimate

guesswork

guesthouse

guest of honor

guest worker

guidebook

guided missile

guide dog

guideline

guidepost

guide rope

guideword

guildhall

guildsman

guild socialism

guilt trip *n.*

guilt-trip *tr.v.*

guinea pig

gullwing

gumball

gum band

gumdrop

gumshoe

gunboat

gunboat diplomacy

gun carriage

gun control

gunfight

gunfire

gunflint

gung ho, gung-ho

gunlock

gunman

gunnysack

gunplay

gunpoint

gunpowder

gunroom

gunrunner

gunship

gunshot

gun-shy

gunslinger

gunsmith

gunstock

gunwale

gutbucket

gut course

gutter ball

guttersnipe
guyliner
gypsum board

H

habeas corpus
habitable zone
habit-forming
hackamore
hacksaw
hackwork
ha-ha, haw-haw
hail-fellow
hail-fellow-well-met
Hail Mary
hailstone
hailstorm
hairball
hair band, hairband
hairbrained
hairbreadth
hairbrush
haircloth
haircut
hairdo
hairdresser
hairdressing

hair follicle
hairline
hairline fracture
hairnet
hair pick
hairpiece
hairpin
hair-raiser
hair-raising
hairsbreadth (hair's-)
hair shirt
hair space
hairsplitting
hair spray, hairspray
hairspring
hairstreak
hair stroke
hairstyle
hair trigger *n.*
hair-trigger *adj.*
hair weave
half-and-half
halfback
half-baked
half bathroom
half binding
half blood, half-blood

half-blooded

half boot

half-bound

half-bred

half-breed

half brother

half-caste

half cock

halfcocked

half-crown

half-dollar

half gainer

halfhearted

half hitch

half-hour

half-length

half-life

half-light

half-mast

half-moon

half nelson

half note

halfpenny

half-pint

halfpipe, half pipe

half-point, half point

half relief

half rest

half rhyme

half shell

half sister

half-slip

half sole *n.*

half-sole *tr.v.*

half-staff

half step

half-timbered

halftime

half title

halftone

half-track

half-truth

half volley

halfway

halfway house

half-wit

hall church

hallmark

Hall of Fame

hall of mirrors

hallway

halo effect

halter-top

ham-handed (-fisted)

hammer and sickle

hammer and tongs

hammerhead

hammerlock

hammerstone

hammertoe

hamstring

hand ax, handax

handbag

handball

handbarrow

hand bell

handbill

handblown, hand-blown

handbook

hand brake

handbreadth (hand's-)

handcar

handcart

handclap

handclasp

handcraft

handcuff

hand drum

handfast

handfasting

handfish

hand glass

handgrip

handgun

handheld, hand-held

handhold

handholding

handkerchief

handlebar

handlebar moustache

hand lens

handmade

handmaid

hand-me-down

handoff

hand organ

handout

handpick

hand press

handprint

hand puppet

handrail

handsaw

hand's-breadth (hand's)

hands down

handset

handshake

hands-off

hands-on

handspike

handspring

handstand

hand-to-hand

hand-to-mouth

hand truck

handwork

handwoven

handwringing (hand)

handwrite

handwriting

handyman

handywoman

hangdog

hanger steak

hang-glide

hang glider

hangman

hangnail

hangout

hangover

hangtag

hang time

hang-up

hanky-panky

happenchance

happenstance

happy camper

happy-go-lucky

happy hour

happy hunting ground

harbormaster

hardback

hardball

hard-bitten

hardboard

hardbody

hard-boil

hard-boiled

hardbound

hard case

hard cider

hard coal

hard copy

hard core *n.*

<u>hardcore</u>, hard-core *adj.*

hard court

hardcover

hard disk

hard drive

hardedge

hard-edged

hard-fisted

hard-handed
hardhat, hard-hat
hardhead
hardheaded
hardhearted
hard-hit
hard-hitting
hard knocks
hard labor
hard landing
hard line
hard news
hard-nosed
hardpan
hard-pressed
hard rock
hard sauce
hardscape
hardscrabble
hard sell
hard-set
hard-shell
hard-spun
hardstand
hardtack
hardtop
hardware

hard wheat
hardwire, hard-wire
hardwood
harebrained, (hair)
harelip
harem pants
harmonic motion
harm's way
harness race
harpoon gun
harvest home
harvestman
harvest moon
harvestwoman
has-been
hash browns
hash house
hash mark
hash slinger
hashtag
hasty pudding
hatband
hatbox
hatchback
hatcheck
hatchet face
hatchet job

hatchet man
hatchway
hate crime
hate mail
hatemonger
hate speech
hat hair
hatpin
hat trick
hate figure
hate preacher
have-not
hawk-eyed
haycock
hay fever
hayfork
hayloft
haymaker
haymow
hayrick
hayride
hayseed
haystack
haywire
hazard light
hazardous waste
headache

headband
headbanger
headboard
headcheese
head cold
head count, headcount
headcounter
headdress
headfast
headfirst
head gate
headgear
headhunt
headhunting
headlamp
headland
headlight
headline
headliner
headlock
headlong
headman
headmaster
head mike
headmistress
head money
headmost

head of state
head-on
headphone
headpiece
headpin
headquarter
headquarters
headrace
head register
headrest
head rhyme
headroom
headsail
headscarf
head sea
headset
headshake
head shop
headshot
headshrinker
headsman
headspace
headspring
headstall
headstand
head start
headstock

headstone
headstream
headstrong
heads up *interj.*
heads-up *adj.*
heads-up display
head-to-head
head trip
head voice
headwaiter
headwaitress
head wall
headwater
headway
headwear
headwind, head wind
headwoman
headword
headwork
health care, healthcare
health food
health insurance
health law
hearing aid
hearing dog
hearing-impaired
hearsay

heartache

heart attack

heartbeat

heartbreak

heartbreaker

heartbreaking

heartbroken

heartburn

heart disease

heart failure

heartfelt

heart-healthy

hearthrug

hearthstone

heartland

heart-lung machine

heart massage

heart rate

heart-rending (heart)

heart-searching

heartsease (heart's-)

heartsick

heartstopper

heart-stricken

heartstring

heartthrob

heart-to-heart

heartwarming

heartwood

heat death

heat engine

heat exchanger

heat exhaustion

heat index

heat island

heat lightning

heatproof

heat prostration

heat pump

heat rash

heat shield

heat sink

heat stroke

heat-treat

heat wave

heave ho *interj.*

heave-ho *n.*

heaven-sent

heavier-than-air

heavy-duty

heavy-footed

heavy-handed

heavy-hearted

heavy hitter

heavy hydrogen
heavy-laden
heavy lifting
heavy metal
heavyset
heavy water
heavyweight
hedge fund
hedgehop
hedgerow
heebie-jeebies
heehaw
heel-and-toe
heelball
heelpiece
heelpost
heeltap
heelwork
heigh-ho
height-to-paper
Heimlich maneuver
heir apparent
heir presumptive
helicopter parent
hellbender
hell-bent, hell bent
hellbox

hellcat
hell-for-leather
hellhole
hellhound
hell-raiser
helmsman
helmsperson
helmswoman
helpmate
helpmeet
helter-skelter
hemline
hemstitch
henceforth
henceforward
henchman
henpeck
hepcat
herbal medicine
herb doctor
herdsman
herdsperson
herdswoman
hereabout
hereafter
hereby
herein

hereinabove
hereinafter
hereinbefore
hereinto
hereof
hereon
hereto
heretofore
hereunto
hereupon
herewith
herky-jerky
heroic couplet
heroic drama
heroic verse
hero worship
herringbone
hex sign
heyday
hiccup, hiccough
hidden agenda
hide-and-seek
hideaway
hidebound
hideout
hidey-hole
higgledy-piggledy

high altar
high-and-mighty
highball
high beam
highbinder
high blood pressure
highborn
highboy
highbred
highbrow
highchair
high-class
high comedy
high command
high commissioner
high-concept
high-count.
high court
high-def
high definition
high-end
higher education
higher law
higher learning
higher-up
high explosive
high fashion

high fidelity

high finance

high-five

highflier, high-flier

high-flown

highflying

high frequency

high gear

high-grade

high ground

highhanded

high hat *n.*

high-hat *tr.v.*

high-hat cymbals (hi-)

high horse

high jinks, hijinks

high jump

highland

highlander

high-level

highlife, high life

highlight

highlighter

high-low

high-minded

high muckamuck

high-necked

high noon

high-pitched

high place

high-powered

high-pressure

high priest

high priestess

high profile

high relief

high-resolution

high-rise

high-risk

high road, highroad

high roller

high school

high seas

high sign

high society

high-sounding

high-speed

high-spirited

high stick *n.*

high-stick *tr.v.*

high-sticking

high street

high-strung

high style

hightail

high tea

high tech *n.*

high-tech, hi-tech *adj.*

high technology

high-tension

high-test

high-ticket

high tide

high-toned

high-top

high treason

high water

high-water mark

highway

highwayman

highway robbery

highwaywoman

high wire

high-wrought

hijack, highjack

hillcrest

hillside

hilltop

himself

hind limb

hindmost

hindquarter

hindsight

hinge joint

hipbone

hip boot

hip bump

hip-hop, hip hop

hip-huggers

hip joint

hip pocket

hippy chick

hip roof (hipped)

hip shot

hired gun

hired hand

hiring hall

hisself

hissy fit

historical linguistics

historical novel

historical present

hit-and-miss

hit-and-run

hitchhike

hitching post

hit list

hit man

hit-or-miss
hit parade
hoarding disorder
hoarfrost
hobbledehoy
hobble skirt
hobbyhorse
hobgoblin
hobnail
hobnob
hockey stick
hockshop
hodgepodge
hoecake
hoedown
hogback
hog heaven
hogtie, hog-tie
hogwash
hog-wild
ho hum *interj.*
ho-hum *adj.*
hoity-toity
holdall
holdback
hold-down
holdfast

holding company
holding pattern
holdout
holdover
holdup
hole-and-corner
hole card
hole in one
hole in the wall
holier-than-thou
hollowware, holloware
hollywood bed
holy day, holyday
holy of holies
holy oil
holy order
holystone
holy terror
holy war
holy water
holy writ
home base
homebody
homebound *n. traveling*
homebound *n. confined*
homeboy
homebred

homebrew, home brew

homebuilder

homebuyer

homecoming

home economics, home ec

home-equity load

home fries

home front

homegirl

homegrown

home invasion

homeland

homemade

homemaker

homeowner

homepage, home page

home plate

home port

home range

homeroom

home rule

home run

homeschool

homesick

homespun

homestand

homestead

homestretch

homestyle

home theater

hometown

home truth

home turf

home video

homework

homing pigeon

honest broker

honest-to-goodness, (to)

honeycomb

honeymoon

honky-tonk

honorable discharge

honorable mention

honor code

honor guard

honor roll

honor society

honor system

hoodmold

hoodwink

hoof-and-mouth disease

hoofbeat

hook and eye

hook-and-ladder truck

hook check
hooknose
hook shot
hookup
hoop skirt
hoosegow
hootchy-kootchy
hope chest
hophead
hopping mad
hopscotch
horizontal bar
hornbook
hornets' nest
horn of plenty
hornpipe
horn-rims
hornswoggle
horror show
horseback
horsehair
horsehide
horselaugh
horseless carriage
horseman
horsemanship
horse opera

horseplay
horseplayer
horsepower
horserace, horse race
horse sense
horseshoe
horse-trading
horsewhip
horsewoman
hospital corner
hostile takeover
hostname
hot air
hotbed
hotblood
hot-blooded
hotbox
hot button
hotcake, hot cake
hotchpot
hotchpotch
hot corner
hot cross bun
hot dog, hotdog *n.*
hot-dog *intr.v.*
hotelkeeper
hot flash

hotfoot	houndstooth check
hothead	hourglass
hotheaded	hour hand
hothouse	hourlong, hour-long
hotline, hot line	house arrest
hotlink	houseboat
hot metal	housebound
hot money	houseboy
hot pack	house brand
hot pepper	housebreak
hot plate	housebreaking
hot pot	house call
hot potato	housecat
hot rod, hot-rod	housecleaning
hot seat	housecoat
hotshot	house detective
hot spot, hotspot	housedress
hot spring	housefather
hot stuff	housegirl
hot ticket	houseguest
hot toddy	household
hot tub	household arts
hot war	householder
hot water	household troops
hot-water bottle	househusband
hot-wire	housekeeper
hot-wired	housekeeping

house league
houselights
housemade
housemaid
houseman
housemaster
housemate
housemistress
housemother
house mouse
house music
house of cards
house officer
house of mirrors
house organ
housepainter (house)
houseparent
house party
houseperson
house physician
houseplant
house-proud
house-raising
houseroom
house seat
housesit
housesitter

house staff
housetop
house trailer
housetrain, house-train
housewares
housewarming
housewife
housewifely
housewifery
housework
housing development
housing project
housing start
hovercraft
howbeit
however
howsoever
hub-and-spoke
hubba-hubba
hubble-bubble
hubcap
huckaback
hue and cry
hugger-mugger
human being
human capital
human-interest

humankind

human nature

human resources

human rights

human shield

humbug

humdinger

humdrum

humpback

hunchback

hundredfold*

hunger strike

hung jury

hung-over, hung over

hung up

hunky-dory

hunt-and-peck

hunter-gatherer

hunter's moon

huntsman

hurdy-gurdy

hurly-burly

hurricane deck

hurricane lamp

hurry-scurry (-skurry)

hurry-up

husbandman

hush-hush

hush money

hush puppy, hushpuppy

husking bee

hybrid vigor

hydraulic fracturing

hydraulic press

hydraulic ram

hydrogen bomb

hydrogen bond

hydrothermal vent

hymnbook, hymn book

hypodermic injection

hypodermic needle

hypodermic syringe

I

ice age

ice ax

ice bag

iceberg lettuce

iceblink

iceboat

icebound

icebox

icebreaker

ice bucket

icecap, ice cap
ice-cold
ice cream
ice-cream chair
ice-cream cone
ice-cream soda
ice cube
iced tea, ice tea
icefall
ice field
ice fish *n.*
ice-fish *intr.v.*
ice floe
ice fog
ice foot
ice-free
ice hockey
icehouse
icemaker
iceman
ice milk
ice needle
ice-out
ice pack
ice pick
ice point
icescape

ice sheet
ice shelf
ice show
ice skate
ice storm
ice water
ice wine
identical rhyme
identity crisis
identity politics
idiot box
idiot light
idiot-proof
idle pulley (idler)
idle wheel
ignition point
ill-advised
ill-being
ill-bred
ill-conceived
ill-considered
ill-defined
ill-disguised
ill-equipped
ill-fated
ill-favored
ill feeling

ill-fitting
ill-founded
ill-gotten
ill humor
ill-mannered
ill nature
ill-natured
ill-starred
ill-tempered
ill-timed
ill-treat
ill-usage
ill-use
ill will
ill-wisher
image-maker
imagesetter
image tube
imaginary number
immoveable feast
immune reaction
immune response
immune system
impact structure
impact zone
imposing stone
imposter syndrome

improper fraction
in-and-in
in-and-out
inasmuch as
in between *prep. & adv.*
in-between *adj.*
inboard
inborn
inbound *adv. & adj.*
inbound *tr.v.*
inbox
inbreathe
inbred
inbreed
inbreeding
inbuilt
inchmeal
incidental music
inclined plane
inclusive of
income bond
income fund
income property
income tax
incoming
incurve
indefinite article

indefinite integral
indefinite pronoun
independent city
independent living
index finger
index fund
index number
India ink
Indian giver
Indian pony
Indian summer
Indian wrestling
India paper
indirect evidence
indirect lighting
indirect object
indirect tax
indoor
indoor-outdoor
indoors
indoor soccer
indraft
indrawn
induced abortion
induced reaction
industrial arts
industrial park

industrial psychology
industrial relations
industrial revolution
industrial-strength
industrial union
industrial waste
indwell
indwelling
inert gas
infant baptism
infantry fighting vehicle
infantryman
infant school
inferiority complex
interior planet
infernal machine
infield
infielder
infighting
infill
inflection point
in-flight
inflow
influence peddling
information age
information technology
informed consent

ingather

ingoing

ingrained

in-group

ingrown

inhaler

inheritance tax

in-home

in-house

injection molding

injection well

injury time

inkblot

inkblot test

inkhorn

in-kind

inkjet printer

inkstand

inkwell

inlaid

inland

in-law

in-law apartment

inlay

inline skate

inner city

inner ear

innersole

innerspring

inner tube

innerwear

innkeeper

input device

inroad

inrush

ins and outs

inseam

inside job

inside of

insider trading

inside track

in situ

insofar

insofar as

insole

insomuch as

insomuch that

inspector general

installation art

installment plan

instant message

instant messaging

instant replay

instead of

instroke
instrument flying
instrument landing
instrument panel
insulin shock
integrated circuit
intellectual property
intelligence quotient
intelligence test
intelligent design
intensive care
intensive care unit
interest group
interior decoration
international law
international relations
intestinal fortitude
inverse function
invert sugar
investment bank
invisible hand
invisible ink
inward dive
in-your-face
ion engine
ion microscope
ion propulsion

ion rocket
Irish bull
Irish coffee
Irish stew
Irish whiskey
ironbound
ironclad
iron cross
iron curtain
iron fist
iron hand
iron horse
ironing board
iron lung
iron maiden
ironman
ironmonger
ironsmith
ironstone
ironware
ironwoman
ironwork
ironworker
ironworks
irregular galaxy
island arc
Italian bread

Italian dressing
Italian sandwich
itty-bitty, itsy-bitsy
ivory tower

J

jack-a-dandy
jackass
jackboot, jack-boot
jack cheese
jack field
jack flag
jackhammer
jackhole
jacking point
jack-in-the-box
jackknife
jackleg
jacklight
jackman
jack-of-all-trades
jack-o'-lantern
jackplane
jackpot
jackscrew
jackshaft
jack squat

jackstay
jackstone
jackstraw
jack-tar, Jack-tar
jack up
Jacob's ladder
jailbait
jailbird
jailbreak
jailhouse
jailhouse lawyer
jam-pack
jam session
jam-up
jarhead
jasper ware, jasperware
jawbone
jawbreaker
jaw-dropping
jawline
jaywalk
jazz dance
jazz-fusion
jazzman
jazz-rock
jellybean
jellyroll

jelly sandal

jerkwater

jerry-build

jerry can

jerry-rig

jet boat

jet engine

jetfighter, jet fighter

jetfoil

jet lag, jetlag

jetliner

jetpack

jetport

jet-propelled

jet propulsion

jet set

jet stream

jewel box

jewel case

Jew's harp, jew's harp

jigger mast

jiggery-pokery

jigsaw puzzle

jim-dandy

jim-jams

jitterbug

job action

jobholder

job-hop

job-hunt

job lot

Job's comforter

job-share

job stick

jock itch

jockstrap, jock strap

jog trot

johnboat

johnnycake

Johnny-come-lately

Johnny-on-the-spot

joint compound

joint probability

joint resolution

joint stock

joint-stock company

joint venture

jollyboat

Jolly Roger

joss house

joss stick

journal box

journey cake

journeyman

journeywork

joypop

joy ride

joystick

judge advocate

judge advocate general

jug band

jugular vein

jug wine

juicehead

jukebox

juke house

juke joint

jump ball

jump bid

jump cut

jumper cable

jump hook

jumping bean

jumping jack

jumping-off place

jump jet

jump-off

jump rope

jump seat

jump shot

jump-start

jump suit

junction box

jungle fever

jungle gym

junior college

junior featherweight

junior flyweight

junior heavyweight

junior high school

junior lightweight

junior middleweight

junior miss

junior varsity

junior welterweight

juniper oil

juniper tar

junk art

junk bond

junk food

junk mail

junkyard

jury nullification

jury-rig

just-folks

justice of the peace

just intonation

juvenile court

juvenile delinquent

K

kaiser roll
kangaroo court
keelboat
keelhaul
keepsake
kettledrum
kettle of fish
keyboard
keycard
key club
key drive
key escrow
keyhole
key money
keynote
keynote address
keynoter
keynote speech
keypad
key pattern
keypunch
key signature
keystone
keystroke

keyway
keyword, key word
kickback
kickball
kickboard
kickboxing
kickoff, kick-off
kickstand
kick-start
kick starter
kick the can
kick turn
kid glove
kidnap
kidney punch
kidney stone
kidskin
kid stuff
killer bee
killing field
killjoy
kilowatt-hour
kindhearted
kindling point
kinetic art
kinetic energy
kinetic friction

kinfolk

kingbolt

kingcraft

kingdom come

kingdom hall

kingmaker

king-of-arms

kingpin

king post

kingside

king-size

kinsfolk

kinsman

kinswoman

kiss-and-tell

kissing cousin

kissing disease

kiss of death

kiss-off

kiss of life

kiss of peace

kit bag

kitchen cabinet

kitchen garden

kitchen police

kitchenware

kiteboard

kiteboarding

kite landboarding

kitesurfing, kite surfing

kith and kin

kitten heel

kitty-cornered

knapsack

knee action

kneeboard

knee breeches

kneecap

knee-deep

knee-high

kneehole

knee jerk *n.*

knee-jerk *adj.*

kneepad

knee sock

<u>knickknack</u> (nicknack)

knife-edge

knifepoint

knight bachelor

knight-errant

knighthead

knit stitch

knitting needle

knitwear

knockabout

knockdown

knockdown-dragout

knock-knee

knockoff

knockout

knothole

know-how

know-it-all

knowledge base

knowledge engineer

know-nothing

knuckle ball, knuckleball

knucklebone

knuckle-duster

knucklehead

knuckle joint

knuckle sandwich

kosher pickle

kosher salt

L

labor-intensive

laborsaving

labor union

lace-curtain

lacework

lackaday

lackluster

lacky band

ladder-back

ladies' man (lady's)

ladies' room

ladyfinger

lady in waiting

lady-killer

ladylike

ladylove

lag screw

laid-back

laid paper

lakebed

lake dwelling

lake effect

lakefront

lakeshore

lakeside

la-la land

lambskin

lamb's wool

lamebrain

lame duck

lampblack

lamplight

lamplighter
lamp oil
lamppost
lampshade
lampworking
lance corporal
lancet arch
lancet window
land art
land bank
landboard
landboarding
land breeze
land bridge
landfall
landfill
landform
land grab
land grant
landholder
landing craft
landing field
landing gear
landing strip
landlady
landline
landlocked

landlord
landlubber
landmark
landmass
land mile
land mine
land office
land-office business
landowner
land-poor
landrace
land reform
landscape
landscape gardener
landside
landslide
landslip
landsman
language arts
language laboratory
lantern jaw
lantern wheel
lap belt
lapboard
lap dance
lap joint
lap robe

lapse rate

laptop

large cap

large-hearted

large-minded

larger than life

large-scale

laser disc, laser disk

laser printer

laser sight

last-born, lastborn

last-ditch

last-gasp

last hurrah

last-in, first-out

last laugh

last minute

last name

last rites

last straw

last word

latchkey

latchkey child

latchstring

latecomer

late-night, late night

lateral pass

late-term

latewood

latex paint

latter-day

lattice crust

latticework

laughing gas

laughingstock

laughline

laugh track

launching pad

launch pad

launch vehicle

laundry list

law-abiding

law and order

lawbreaker

law clerk

lawgiver

lawmaker

lawman

law merchant

lawn bowling

lawn mower, lawnmower

lawn tennis

law of averages

law of inertia

131

law of parsimony

law of thermodynamics

lawsuit

layabout

layaway

layback

lay figure

layman

layoff

layout

layover

layperson

lay reader

lay-up

laywoman

lazybones

lazy eye

lazy Susan

lazy tongs

lead balloon

leaderboard

leading edge

leading tone

lead line

leadoff

lead-out

lead pencil

lead poisoning

leadsman

lead-time

lead-up

leaf scar

leaf spring

leakproof

lean-to

leapfrog

leap second

leap year

learning curve

learning disability

learning-disabled

leaseback

leasehold

leash law

leastways

leastwise

leatherneck

leatherwear

leatherwork

leave of absence

leave-taking

ledger board

ledger line

leeboard

lee shore
leeway
left-brained
left face
left field
left fielder
left-hand
left-handed
left-hander
leftmost
leftover
left wing, Left Wing
legal age
legal aid
legal holiday
legal pad
legal separation
legal-size
legal tender
leg curl
legman
leg-of-mutton
legroom
leg warmer, legwarmer
legwork
leisure suit
leisurewear

lemonade
lemon drop
lemon law
lemon stick
lending library
lenticular galaxy
leopardskin
lesser ape
letdown, let-down
lethal injection
letter bomb
letterbox
letter carrier
letterform
letterhead
letterman
letter of credence
letter of credit
letter of intent
letter-perfect
letterpress
letter-quality
letters of administration
letters of marque
letters patent
letters testamentary
letup

levelheaded

leveling rod

level of significance

leveraged buyout

liberal arts

liberty cap

library science

license plate

lickety-split

lickspittle

licorice stick

lie detector

liegeman

life-and-death

life belt

lifeblood

lifeboat

life buoy

life care, lifecare

life coach

life cycle

life expectancy

life form

lifeguard

lifehack, life hack

life history

life insurance

life jacket

lifelike

lifeline

life list

lifelong

life mask

life-or-death

life preserver

life raft

lifesaver

life science

life-size

lifespan, life span

lifestyle

life support *n.*

life-support *adj.*

life-support system

lifetime

lifeway

lifework

life zone

liftgate

lifting body

liftoff

light board

light bread

light breeze

light bulb
light-emitting diode
lighter-than-air
lightface
light-fingered
light-footed
light-handed
lightheaded
lighthearted
light heavyweight
lighthouse
light meter
light-minded
lightning arrester
lightning chess
lightning rod
light opera
light pen
lightplane
light pollution
lightproof
light rail
light reflex
light sail
lightship
light show
lights out

light-struck
light water
lightweight
lightwood
light year
like-minded
lily-livered
lily-white
limeade
limekiln
limelight
limited access highway
limited edition
limited liability company
limited partnership
limited war
linchpin, lynchpin
linear accelerator
linebacker
line breeding
linecaster
line cut
line dance
line drawing
line drive
line engraving
line item

line-item veto
lineman
line of credit
line officer
line of force
line of scrimmage
line of sight
line-out
line printer
linerboard
liner notes
line score
linesman
line squall
line storm
lineswoman
lineup
linguistic atlas
linguistic form
linguistic geography
linkup
linseed oil
lip gloss
lip liner, lipliner
lip-lock
lip-read
lip reading

lip service
lip-smacking
lipstick
lip-synch, lip-sync
liquid air
liquid crystal
liquid-crystal display
liquid measure
list price
listserver
litmus paper
litmus test
litterbag
litterbug
littermate
little finger
little magazine
little slam
little theater
little toe
liveblog
live-forever
live-in
live load
livelong
live parking
liver spot

liveryman
livery stable
live steam
livestock
live wire
living death
living room
living trust
living unit
living wage
living will
loadmaster
loaf bread
loan shark
loansharking
loanword
lobsterman
lobster pot
lobster shift
lobsterwoman
local anesthesia
local anesthetic
local color
local option
lockdown
locker room *n.*
locker-room *adj.*

lockkeeper
lockmaster
locknut, lock nut
lock-on
lockout
lockset
locksmith
lockstep
lockstitch, lock stitch
lockup
logbook
loggerhead
logjam
log line
logon
logroll
logrolling
loincloth
lollipop, lollypop
lollygag, lallygag
lone hand
lone wolf
longboat
longbow
long-day
long distance *n.*
long-distance *adj.*

long division

long-drawn-out

long face

long game

long green

longhair

long-haired, longhaired

longhand

long haul

longheaded, long-headed

longhouse, long house

long johns

long jump

longline

long-liner

longlist

long-lived

longneck

long-playing

long-range

long run

longshore

longshoreman

long shot

long-sighted

long-standing (long)

long-suffering

long suit

long-term

longtime

long ton

long-wasted

long wave

long-winded

look-alike, lookalike

look-in

looking glass

lookout

look-see

lookup

loony bin

loophole

loose cannon

loose end

loose-jointed

loose-leaf

loose-lipped

loosey-goosey

lop-eared

lopsided

lose-lose

loss leader

loss ratio

lost and found (-and-)

lotus-eater
lotus land
lotus position
loudmouth
loudspeaker
lounge car
lounge lizard
lounge music
loungewear
love affair
love apple
love beads
lovebirds
love child
love feast
love handles
love-in
love knot
love life
lovelock
lovemaking
love seat, loveseat
lovesick
lovey-dovey
loving cup
low-ball, lowball
low beam

low blood pressure
low blow
lowborn
lowboy
lowbred
lowbrow
low-cal
low-carb
low-class
low comedy
low country
low-down, lowdown
low-end
lowercase
lowercase letter
lower class
lowerclassman
lower criticism
lower world
lowest terms
low-fi, lo-fi
low fidelity
low frequency
low gear
low-grade
low-hanging fruit
low-key

lowland

lowlander

low-level

lowlife

lowlight

lowlights

low-minded

low-necked, low-neck

low-pitched

low-pressure

low profile

low relief

low-rent

low-resolution

lowrider (low-) (low)

low-rise

low road

low-tech

low-ticket

low tide

low water

lubber line (lubber's)

lubber's hole

lug nut

lukewarm

lumberjack

lumberman

lumberyard

lump sum

lunar month

lunerscape

lunar year

lunatic fringe

lunchbox

lunchmeat

lunchroom

lunchtime

lunkhead

lusterware

lying-in

lymph node

lynch law

lynchpin

lynx-eyed

M

macebearer

machine bolt

machine finish

machine gun *n.*

machine-gun *tr.v.*

machine language

machine pistol

machine-readable

machine screw

machine shop

machine tool

machine translation

machine-wash

Mach number (mach)

mackerel sky

madcap

made-to-order

made-up

madhouse

madman

mad money

magical realism

magic bullet

magic lantern

magic number

magic square

magic word

magnetic card

magnetic compass

magnetic core

magnetic disk

magnetic field

magnetic flux

magnetic force

magnetic head

magnetic lines of force

magnetic mine

magnetic needle

magnetic north

magnetic north pole

magnetic pole

magnetic recording

magnetic south

magnetic south pole

magnetic storm

magnetic tape

magnet school

magnifying glass

mag wheel

maidenhead

maiden name

maiden over

maid in waiting

maid of honor

maidservant

mailbag

mailbox

mail call

mail carrier

mail drop

mailed fist

mailman

mail order

mailroom

mailwoman

main chance

main clause

main deck

main drag

mainframe

mainland

mainline *v.*

main line *n.*

main man

mainmast

main royalmast

mainsail

mainsheet

mainspring

main squeeze

mainstay

mainstream

main street

maintop

main topmast

main topsail

main verb

main yard

major general

majority leader

majority rule

major league *n.*

major-league *adj.*

major medical

major order

major party

major premise

major scale

major suit

make-believe

make-do

makefast

make-or-break

makeover

makeshift

makeup, make-up

makeweight

make-work

male chauvinist

malice aforethought

malicious mischief

mall walking

malted milk

malt liquor

malt sugar

malt whiskey

mama's boy
man about town
managed care
man-at-arms
man-child
mandarin collar
maneater
man Friday
manhandle
manhole
man-hour
manhunt
manifest destiny
Manila paper
man in the street
mankind
manmade, man-made
man of God
man of letters
man of the cloth
man of the hour
man of the world
man-of-war
man on horseback
manor house
manpower
mansard roof

manservant
manslaughter
manslayer
mantelpiece
mantelshelf
manteltree
man-to-man
mantrap
manual alphabet
manual training
manufactured gas
manufactured home
man-year
manyfold
many-sided
maple sugar
maple syrup
mapmaker
maraschino cherry
marble cake
marching orders
marchland
march-past
mare's nest
mariner's compass
markdown
market basket

market economy
market fund
market garden
market order
marketplace
market price
market research
market share
market timing
market value
marksman
markswoman
markup
markup language
marlinespike
marriage of convenience
marsh gas
marshland
martial art
martial law
mashed potatoes
masked ball
masking tape
masonry cement
massage parlor
mass extinction
mass hysteria

mass-market
mass medium
mass murderer
mass-produce
mass production
master-at-arms
master bedroom
master class
master key
master mason
mastermind
master of ceremonies
masterpiece
master plan
master race
master's degree
master sergeant
masterstroke
masterwork
masthead
mastoid bone
matchboard
matchbook
matchbox
matchlock
matchmaker
match play

match point
matchstick
matchup
materials science
matron of honor
matter of course
matter-of-fact
maulstick, mahlstick
Maypole, maypole
mazel tov, mazal tov
meadowland
meal ticket
mealtime
mealy-mouthed
mean-spirited
meantime
meanwhile
meatball
meathead
meat hook
meatloaf, meat loaf
meat market
meatpacking
medal play
media event
medical examiner
medical jurisprudence

medicine ball
medicine bundle
medicine dance
medicine man
medicine show
medicine woman
medium frequency
medium of exchange
meet and greet
meetinghouse
Melba toast
melon dome
meltdown
melting point
melting pot
meltwater
memorial park
menfolk
men's room
menswear, men's wear
mental age
mental block
mental health
mental telepathy
merchant marine
merchant mariner
mercy killing

mercy rule

mercy seat

merit system

merry-andrew

merry-go-round

merrymaking

merry widow

meshwork

mess hall

mess jacket

mess kit

messmate

metal detector

metalhead

metallic bond

metalware

metalwork

metalworking

meteor shower

meter maid

me time

metoo, me-too

metric mile

metric system

metric ton

Mickey Finn

microwave background

microwave bomb

microwave oven

middle age

middle-aged

middle class

middle distance

middle ear

middle ground

middleman

middle management

middle name

middle-of-the-road

middle school

middle term

middleware

middleweight

middy blouse

midfield

midiron

midland

midlevel

midlevel provider

midlife

midlife crisis

midline

midlist

midmorning

midmost
midnight sun
midpoint
midrange
midrib
midriff
mid-rise
midsection
midship
midshipman
midsize, mid-size
midsole
midstream
midsummer
midterm
midtown
midway
midweek
midwife
midwifery
midwinter
midyear
might-have-been
milepost
milestone
military attaché
military intelligence

military law
military police
military science
milk-and-water
milk chocolate
milk glass
milkmaid
milkman
milk of magnesia
milk run
milkshake, milk shake
milksop
milk toast
milk tooth
millboard
milldam
mill end
mill finish
millpond
millrace
millrun *n.*
mill-run *adj.*
millstone
millstream
mill wheel
millwork
millwright

147

milquetoast
mincemeat
mind-altering
mind-bending
mind-blowing
mind-body
mind-boggling
mind-expanding
mind game
mind reading
mindscape
mindset, mind-set
mind's eye
mine detector
minefield
minelayer
mineral kingdom
mineral oil
mineral tar
mineral water
mineral wool
mineshaft
minesweeper
mineworker
miniature golf
minimum wage
minimumweight

minority leader
minor league *n.*
minor-league *adj.*
minor-leaguer
minor order
minor party
minor planet
minor premise
minor scale
minor suit
minor term
minstrel show
mint julep
mintmark
minus sign
minute hand
minuteman
minute steak
miracle drug
miracle play
mirror image
mirror site
mischief-maker
misery index
mishmash
missing link
missing mass

misty-eyed
miter box
miter joint
miter square
mixed bag
mixed doubles
mixed drink
mixed economy
mixed grill
mixed marriage
mixed martial art
mixed media
mixed metaphor
mixed number
mixed-up
mixed-use
mix-up, mixup
mobcap
mobile home
mobile phone
mocktail
mock turtle soup
mockup, mock-up
modern art
modern dance
modern pentathlon
moldboard

molecular biology
molecular clock
molecular formula
molecular medicine
molecular profiling
molecular weight
molehill
moleskin
mollycoddle
Molotov cocktail
mom-and-pop
moment of inertia
moment of truth
mommy track
monetary unit
moneybag
moneybags
money belt
moneychanger
moneygrubber
moneylender
money machine
moneymaking
moneyman
money market
money of account
money order

money player

money shot

money supply

money trail

monkey bars

monkey blood

monkey business

monkey jacket

monkeyshine

monkey wrench

monk's cloth

mood disorder

moo juice

moonbeam

mooncake, moon cake

mooncalf

moonchild

moon-eyed

moon-faced

moonlight

moonlit

moonquake

moonrise

moonroof

moonscape

moonset

moonshine

moonstone

moonstruck

moonwalk

moorland

moot court

mopboard

mop-up

moral hazard

morality play

morning-after pill

morning breath

morning sickness

morning star

Morris chair

Morse code

mortal sin

mortarboard

mosh pit

mosquito boat

mosquito net

mossback

mossgrown

moss-trooper

most-favored-nation

mothball

moth-eaten

motherboard

mother country

mother figure

motherhouse

mother-in-law

motherland

mother lode

mother-of-pearl

mother superior

mother tongue

mother wit

motion picture

motion sickness

motorbike

motorboat

motorbus

motorcar

motorcoach

motor court

motorcycle

motor drive

motor home

motor inn

motor lodge

motorman

motor mouth

motor pool

motor scooter

motor vehicle

motorway

mottled enamel

mountain bike

mountain climbing

mountain dew

mountain range

mountain sickness

mountainside

mountaintop

mourners' bench

mousepad, mouse pad

mousetrap

mousseline

mouthfeel

mouth harp

mouth organ

mouthpiece

mouthwash

mouthwatering

movable feast

movable type

movement therapy

mover and shaker

moviegoer

moviemaker

moving picture

moving sidewalk

muckrake

mucous membrane

muddle-headed

mud flat

mudflow

mudguard

mudroom

mudsill

mudslide

mudslinger

muffin top

mug shot

mugwump

muleskinner

mulligan stew

multiple star

mumblecore

mumblety-peg

mumbo jumbo (mumbo-)

mummy bag

municipal bond

Murphy's Law

musclebound (muscle-)

muscle car

muscleman, muscle man

muscle shirt

muscular dystrophy

muscular system

museum piece

mushroom cloud

musical chairs

musical comedy

musical saw

music box

music drama

music hall

music of the spheres

music video

mustard gas

mustard oil

mustard plaster

muster roll

must-have

must-read

must-see

muttonchops

mutual fund

mutual insurance

muzzleloader

myself

mystery play

mythmaker

N

nail bed
nail biter, nailbiter
nailbrush
nail file
nail fold
nail polish
nail scissors
nail set
naked eye
naked option
namby-pamby
name brand
name-calling
name-check
name day
name-drop
name of the game
nameplate
namesake
nanny goat
nanny state
naptime
narrow-bodied
narrowcast
narrow gauge
narrow-minded

nastygram
national bank
national debt
national forest
national income
national monument
national park
national seashore
nation-state
native-born
natural-born
natural capital
natural childbirth
natural food
natural gas
natural history
natural language
natural law
natural resource
natural science
natural virtue
nature trail
nautical mile
naval architect
naval stores
navel-gazing
Neanderthal man

Neapolitan ice cream

near beer

nearby

near Earth asteroid

near Earth object

near miss

near point

near rhyme

nearshore

nearsighted

nearsightedness

near-term

near thing

neckband

neckerchief

necklace

neckline

neck of the woods

neckpiece

necktie

neckwear

needlecraft

needlepoint

needle valve

needlewoman

needlework

ne'er-do-well

negative capability

negative pressure

negative space

nerve agent

nerve center

nerve gas

nerve impulse

nerve net

nerve-racking (-wracking)

nerve trunk

nest egg

nesting doll

net asset value

netback

netbook

netherworld (nether)

netkeeper

netminder

netroots

nettlesome

net ton

network

neutral ground

neutral spirits

neutral zone

neutron bomb

neutron star

never-ending
nevermore
never-never land
nevertheless
new blood
newborn
newcomer
new-fashioned
newfound
newlywed
new moon
news agency
newsboy
newscast
news conference
newsdealer
news flash
newsgathering
newsgirl
newsgroup
newshound
newsletter
newsmagazine
newsmaker
newsman
newsmonger
newspaper

newspapering
newspaperman
newspaperwoman
newspeak
newsperson
newsprint
newsreel
news release
newsroom
newsstand
newsweekly
newswire
newswoman
newsworthy
new town
new wave
next door
next friend
next of kin
nickel-and-dime
nickel silver
nicknack
nickname
night-blind
night blindness
nightcap
nightclothes

nightclub

night court

nightdress

nightfall

nightglow

nightgown

night latch

night letter

nightlife

night-light

nightlong

nightmare

night-night (nighty-)

night owl

nightrider

nightscape

night school

nightshade

night shift, nightshift

nightshirt

nightspot

nightstand

nightstick

night table

night terror

nighttime

night vision

nightwalker

night watch

night watchman

nightwear

niminy-piminy

nincompoop

nine ball

nine days' wonder

ninepin

nip and tuck

nip-up

nitpick

nitpicky

nitrogen cycle

nitty-gritty

nitwit

noble gas

nobleman

noble metal

noblewoman

nobody

no-brainer

no-fault

no fewer than

no-fly zone

no-frills

no-go

no-good

no-hit

no-hitter

no-holds-barred

nohow

noisemaker

noise masking

noise pollution

no-load

no-lose

no man's land

nonce word

nonetheless

no-no

noonday

no one

noontide

noontime

normal curve

normal fault

normal school

northbound

northern lights

northland

nosebag

noseband

nosebleed

nose candy

nose cone

nosedive *n.*

nose-dive *intr.v.*

nose guard

nose job

nosepiece

nose ring

nose tackle

no-show

notary public

notchback

notebook

notepad

notepaper

noteworthy

no-trump

notwithstanding

nowadays

noway

nowhere

nowheresville

no-win

nowise

nuclear age

nuclear energy

nuclear family

nuclear force

nuclear physics

nuclear power

nuclear reaction

nuclear reactor

nuclear weapon

nuclear winter

nuisance tax

null character

number cruncher

number line

number one

numbers game

number sign

number system

number theory

numerical analysis

numerical control

numerical value

numskull, numbskull

nursemaid

nurse-midwife

nurse practitioner

nursery rhyme

nursery school

nurse's aide

nursing home

nutcase, nut case

nutcracker

nut house

nutjob, nut job

nutmeat

nut pick, nutpick

nuts and bolts

nutshell

O

oak leaf cluster

oarlock

oarsman

oarswoman

oatcake

oatmeal

object ball

object code

object lesson

obligatory bill

oblique angle

oblique triangle

obstacle course

obtuse angle

oceanfront

oceangoing

Ockham's razor

octane number
oddball
odd job
odd lot
odd-man
odd man out
odds and ends
oddsmaker
odds-on
off-air
off and on, off-and-on
offbeat
off-brand
off-Broadway
off chance
off-color
off-duty
off-guard
offhand
off-hour
office boy
office girl
officeholder
office park
officer of the day
off-key
off-label

off-limits
offline, off-line
offload, off-load
off-off-Broadway
off-peak
off-piste
off-price
offprint
off-putting
off-road
offscouring
offscreen
off-season
offset
offset printing
offshoot
offshore
offside
offsite
off-speed
offspring
offstage
off-the-books
off-the-cuff
off the grid
off-the-rack
off-the-record

off-the-shelf

off-the-wall

off-track

off-track betting

off year

oftentimes

ohmmeter

oil cake

oilcan

oilcloth

oil color

oil field

oil paint

oil painting

oil pan

oilpaper

oil patch

oil sand

oil shale

oilskin

oil slick

oilstone

oil well

okey-dokey

old boy

old-boy network

oldfangled (old-)

old-fashioned

old-field

old girl

old-girl network

old-growth

old guard

old hand

old hat

old lady

old-line

old maid

old man

old master

old money

old moon

old school *n.*

old-school *adj.*

old school tie

old snow

old-time

old-timer

old wives' tale

olive branch

olive oil

on-again, off-again

on-air

on-base percentage

onboard, on-board

onboarding

on-brand

once-over

oncoming

one another

one-armed bandit

one-bagger

one-base hit

one-dimensional

one-finger keyboard

one-handed

one-liner

one-man

one-night stand

one-note

one-off

one-on-one

one-piece

oneself

one-shot

one-sided

one-size-fits-all

one-step

one-stop

one-time

one-time pad

one-to-one

one-touch

one-track

one-trick pony

one-two punch

one-up

one-upmanship

one-way

one-way mirror

one-woman

ongoing

onion dome

onionskin

onion snow

onlay

online, on-line

onload

onlooker

onrush

onscreen, on-screen

onset

onshore

onside

onside kick

onsite

onslaught

onstage

on-stream
on-the-job
on-the-record
on-the-scene
onto
onward
opaque projector
op art, Op Art
open-access
open admissions
open adoption
open-air
open-and-shut
open-ballot voting
open city
open classroom
open cluster
open court
open door
open-end
open-ended
open-end wrench
open enrollment
open-eyed
open-faced
openhanded
openhearted

open-hearth
open-heart surgery
open house
open letter
open listing
open loop
open market
open marriage
open meeting law
open mike
open-minded
open-mouthed
open season
open secret
open sesame
open shop
open-source
open stock
open system
open universe
openwork
opera glass
operagoer
opera house
operating expenditure
operating expense
operating room

operating system

operations research

opposite field

opposite number

optical art

optical computer

optical disc, optical disk

optical fiber

optical illusion

optical resonator

optical scanner

optical tweezers

optic nerve

oral contraceptive

oral history

oral hygiene

oral tradition

orangeade

orange stick

orbital velocity

order arms

order of battle

order of business

order of magnitude

order of the day

ordinary seaman

organ grinder

organized crime

organ point

organ transplant

Oriental rug

original sin

origination fee

orphan disease

orthodox sleep

orthogonal projection

oscillating circuit

oscillating universe

osmotic pressure

other-directed

other half

other than

otherwise

otherworld

otherworldly

ourself

ourselves

out and away

out-and-out

out-and-outer

outback

outbalance

outbid

outboard

outboard motor

outbound

outbox

outbreak

outbreed

outbreeding

outbuilding

outburst

outcall

outcast

outclass

outcome

outcompete

outcrop

outcross

outcry

outcurve

outdate

outdated

outdistance

outdo

outdoor

outdoors

outdoorsman

outdoorswoman

outdoorsy

outer ear

outermost

outer planet

outer space

outerwear

outface

outfall

outfield

outfielder

outfit

outflank

outflow

outfox

out-front

outgas

outgeneral

outgo

outgoing

outgroup, out-group

outgrow

outgrowth

outguess

outgun

outhaul

outhouse

outing flannel

outland

outlander

outlast

outlaw

outlawry

outlay

outlier

outline

outline font

outlive

outlook

out loud

outlying

outman

outmaneuver

outmatch

outmigration

outmoded

outmost

outmuscle

outnumber

out of

out-of-body

out-of-bounds

out-of-court

out-of-date

out-of-door

out-of-doors

out-of-pocket

out-of-state

out-of-stater

out-of-the-way

out-of-touch

out-of-town

out-of-towner

outpace

outpatient

outperform

outplace

outplacement

outplay

outpoint

outpoll

outpost

outpour

outpouring

output

output device

outrace

outrage

outran

outrange

outrank

outreach

outride

outrider

outrigger

outright

outrode

outrun

outscore

outsell

outset

outshine

outshoot

outside

outside of

outsider

outsider art

outsight

outsize

outskirt

outsmart

outsoar

outsold

outsole

outsource

outspend

outspoken

outspread

outstand

outstanding

outstare

outstation

outstay

outstood

outstretch

outstrip

outstroke

outtake

outtalk

outthink

outthrust

outturn

outvote

outwait

outward

outward-bound

outwardly

outwash

outwear

outweigh

outwent

outwit

outwore

outwork

outworn

outyear

oval window

ovenproof

ovensafe
ovenware
overabundance
overachieve
overact
overactive
overaggressive
overall
overalls
overambitious
overanxious
overarch
overarching
overarm
overassess
overate
overawe
overbalance
overbear
overbearing
overbid
overbite
overblouse
overblow
overblown *adj. excessive*
overblown *adj. bloom*
overboard

overbook
overbore
overborne
overbought
overbuild
overburden
overbuy
overcall
overcame
overcapacity
overcapitalize
overcast
overcastting
overcautious
overcharge
overclass
overcloud
overcoat
overcoating
overcome
overcommit
overcompensate
overconfident
overcorrect
overcritical
overcrop
overcrowd

overdevelop

overdevelopment

overdiagnosis

overdo

overdog

overdominance

overdosage

overdose

overdraft

overdraw

overdress

overdrive

overdub

overdue

overeager

overeat

overemphasize

overestimate

overexert

overexpose

overextend

overfamiliar

overfatigue

overfeed

overfill

overfish

overflight

overflow

overfly

overgarment

overglaze

overgraze

overgrow

overgrowth

overhand

overhand knot

overhang

overhaul

overhead

overhead projector

overhear

overheat

overhit

overhung

overhydrate

overhype

overinduldge

overissue

overjoy

overkill

overladen

overlaid

overlain

overland

overlap
overlay
overleaf
overleap
overlearn
overlie
overload
overlong
overlook
overlord
overman
overmaster
overmatch
overmedicate
overmuch
overnight
overnight bag
overnighter
overoptimistic
overpass
overpay
overpersuade
overplay
overplus
overpopulate
overpopulation
overpower

overpowering
overpraise
overprescribe
overpressure
overprice
overprint
overpriviledge
overprize
overproduce
overproof
overproportion
overprotect
overqualified
overran
overrate
overrcach
overreact
overrefine
overregulate
overrepresented
override
overriding
overripe
overrule
overrun
oversaw
overscale

overscore
oversea
overseas
overseas cap
oversee
overseed
overseer
oversell
oversensitive
overset
oversew
oversexed
overshadow
overshirt
overshoe
overshoot
overshot
oversight
oversimplify
oversize
overskirt
oversleep
oversold
oversoul
overspecialize
overspend
overspill

overspread
overstaff
overstate
overstay
oversteer
overstep
overstimulate
overstock
overstory
overstrain
overstress
overstretch
overstride
overstrung
overstuff
oversubscribe
oversupply
overtake
overtax
over-the-counter
over-the-hill
over-the-top
overthrow
overthrust fault
overtime
overtire
overtone

overtone singing
overtook
overtop
overtrade
overtrain
overtrick
overtrump
overturn
overuse
overvalue
overview
overvote
overwear
overweary
overweening
overweigh
overweight
overwind
overwinter
overwithhold
overwore
overwork
overworn
overwound
overwrite
overwrought
overzealous

own brand
own goal
oxbow
oxbow lake
oxtail
oxygen mask
oxygen tent
oyster bed
oyster cracker
oysterman
ozone hole
ozone layer

P

paddleboard
pace car
pace lap
pacemaker
pacesetter
package store
pack animal
packet switching
packhorse
pack ice
packinghouse
packman
pack rat

packsack

packsaddle

packthread

pack train

paddleball

paddleboard

paddleboat

paddle wheel

paddle wheeler

paddy field

paddy wagon

padlock

pageboy

pagejack

page-turner

page view

painkiller

painstaking

paintball

paintbrush

painted lady

pair bond

pale-dry

paleface

palette knife

pallbearer

palm oil

palm sugar

palmtop

palsy-walsy

Panama hat

pan and scan

pan-broil

pancake

pancake landing

panda car

panel discussion

panel truck

pan fish

<u>pan-fry</u>, panfry

panhandle *v. to beg*

panhandle n. *part of pan*

panic attack

panic button

panic disorder

panic-stricken

panpipe

<u>pantsuit</u>, pants suit

pantyhose, panty hose

pantywaist

papal gentleman

paperback

paperboard

paperbound

paperboy
paper clip
paper cutter
papergirl
paperhanger
paperknife
paper mache
papermaking
paper-thin
paper tiger
paper trail
paper-train
paperweight
paperwork
parabolic antenna
parabolic mirror
parachute dome
parachute spinnaker
paradoxical sleep
paraffin wax
parallel bars
parallel computing
parallel cousin
parallel processing
parallel universe
parcel post
parental leave

parent company
parent language
par excellence
parfait glass
paring knife
parking brake
parking lot
parking meter
parking orbit
parkland
parkway
parlor car
parlor game
parlor grand
parochial school
parquet circle
particle accelerator
particle beam
particleboard (particle)
particulate matter
parting shot
part of speech
part song
part-time
partway
party animal
partygoer

party line

party pooper (party-)

party wall

paschal lamb

passage grave

passageway

passagework

pass-along, passalong

passbook

passed ball

passenger virus

passerby, passer-by

pass-fail

passing note

passing shot

passive immunity

passive recreation

passive resistance

passive restraint

passive smoke

passive transfer

passive transport

passkey

pass pattern

pass phrase

passport

pass rush

pass-through

password

pasteboard

pastedown

paste-up

past master

pastureland

PA system

patch cord

patch pocket

patch test

patchwork

patent leather

patent office

patent pending

paternity leave

paternity test

pathbreaker

pathbreaking

pathetic fallacy

pathfinder

pathname

pathway

patriarchal cross

patrol boat

patrol car

patrolman

patrol torpedo boat

patrol wagon

patrolwoman

patron saint

patternmaker (pattern)

patty-cake

pawnbroker

pawnshop

pawn ticket

payback

paycheck

payday

pay dirt

pay equity

payload

paymaster

payoff

payout

pay-per-view

pay phone

payroll, pay roll

payroll tax

pay station

paywall

peace dividend

peacekeeper

peacekeeping

peacemaker

peacenik

peace offering

peace officer

peace pipe

peace sign

peacetime

pea coat, peacoat

pea jacket

peak flow meter

peak oil

peanut brittle

peanut butter

peanut gallery

peanut oil

pearl diver

Pearly Gates

peashooter

pea soup

peat bog

peat moss

pecking order

pedal keyboard

pedal piano

pedal point

pedal pushers

peekaboo

peeping Tom
peepshow, peep show
peep sight
peer pressure
peer-to-peer network
peewee
pegboard
peg leg
Peking man
Pele's hair
Pele's tears
pell-mell, pellmell
penal code
penalty area
penalty box
penalty kick
penalty kill
penalty killer
penalty shot
penalty spot
pen-based
pencil pusher
pen computer
penholder
penknife
penlight
penman

pen name
penny ante
penny loafer
penny pinching
pennyweight
pennywhistle (penny)
penny-wise, pennywise
pennyworth
pen pal
pen point
pen register
pension plan
penstock
penthouse
people mover
people of color
people of interest
pepper-and-salt
pepperbox
peppercorn
pepper game
pepper mill
pepper pot
peppershaker
pepper spray
pep pill
pep talk

perching bird

percussion cap

percussion instrument

per diem

performance art

Periodic Table

permanent magnet

permanent press

permanent tooth

per mil, per mill

perpetual calendar

perpetual motion

perp walk

persistent train

persona grata

personal care

personal computer

personal effects

personal foul

personality test

personal pronoun

personal property

personal watercraft

persona non grata

person of color

person of interest

person-to-person

pesthole

pest house

petit four

petit jury, petty jury

petri dish

petroleum ether

petroleum jelly

petting zoo

petty cash

petty larceny

petty officer

phantom limb

phased array

phasedown

phase-in

phase inverter

phase microscope

phaseout

phase rule

phase shift

philosophers' stone

phone card

phone tag

phonetic alphabet

phony-baloney (phoney-)

photobomb

photocopier

photocopy
photoelectric cell
photoelectric effect
photo finish
photoflash
photoflood
photo-offset
photo op
photo opportunity
phrase book
phrasemaker
physical education
physical therapy
physician assistant
piano bar
pianoforte
piano hinge
piano roll
pick and choose
pick-and-roll
pickax, pickaxe
picket fence
picket line
picklock
pick-me-up
pickoff
pickpocket

pickproof
pickup
pick-up stick
pickup truck
picture disc
picture hat
picture-perfect
picture puzzle
picture tube
picture window
piece goods
piecemeal
piece of eight
piecework
pie chart
pied piper
pie-eyed
piehole
pier glass
pig bed
pigboat
pigeon breast
pigeonhole
pigeon-toed
piggyback
piggy bank
pigheaded

pig iron
pig Latin
pig lead
pig-out
pigpen
pigskin
pigsty
pigtail
pikestaff
pile driver
pileup, pile-up
pilgrim bottle
pillbox
pillow block
pillow book
pillowcase
pillow lace
pillow lava
pillowslip
pillow talk
pilot balloon
pilot bread
pilot burner
pilot cell
pilot engine
pilothouse
pilot lamp

pilot light
pima cotton
pinball
pinball machine
pinch bar
pinchbeck
pinchcock
pinch effect
pinch-hit
pinchpenny
pinch runner
pin curl
pincushion
pinecone
pineland
pine needle
pine nut
pinesap
pine straw
pine tar
pinewood
pinfeather
pinfold
pinhead
pinhole
pink-collar
pinkeye

pinking shears
pink lady
pink slip
pin money
pinpoint
pinpoint oxford
pinprick
pins and needles
pinsetter
pinstripe, pin stripe
pintsize
pinup
pinwheel
pinwrench
pipe bomb
pipe clay
pipe cleaner
pipe dream
pipe fitter
pipefitting
pipeline
pipe organ
pipestone
pipe wrench
pip-squeak
pistol grip
pistol-whip

piston ring
piston rod
pitapat
pit boss
pitch accent
pitch-black
pitchblende
pitch-dark
pitched battle
pitched roof
pitchfork
pitchman
pitchout
pitch-perfect
pitch pine
pitch pipe
pitchpole
pitchstone
pitfall
pith helmet
pitman
pitsaw, pit saw
pit stop
pitter-patter
placebo effect
placeholder
place kick

place mat
placer mining
place setting
plainchant
plainclothes (plain-)
plainclothesman (man)
plain-Jane
plain-laid
plainsman
plainsong
plainspoken
plaintext, plain text
plain vanilla
plain weave
Planck's constant
plane angle
plane geometry
planeload
planeside
plane table
planet wheel
planter's punch
plant kingdom
plantsman
plasma ball
plasmablast
plasma cell

plasma tail
plasterboard
plaster cast
plaster of Paris
plasterwork
plastic explosive
plastic strain
plastic surgery
plastic wrap
plate anemometer
plate glass
plate proof
plate tectonics
platform bed
platform scale
platform tennis
platinum blond
platoon sergeant
play-act
play-action pass
playback
playbill
playbook
playboy
play-by-play
play clock
playdate

player piano

playfellow

playgirl

playground

playhouse

playing card

playing field

playlist, play list

playmaker

playmate

playoff, play-off

playpen

playroom

playsuit

play therapy

plaything

playwear

playwright

playwritng

play yard

plea bargain, plea-bargain

pleasure principle

pleated sheet

plein air, plein-air

plenary indulgence

plot line, plotline

plowback

plowboy

plowman

plowshare

plow steel

plug board

plug-compatible

plug-in

plumb bob

plumber's helper

plumber's snake

plumb line

plumb rule

plum pudding

plural marriage

plus fours

plush toy

plus/minus

plus sign

plus-size

plywood

poboy, po-boy, po'boy

pocket battleship

pocket billiards

pocketbook

pocket borough

pocket bread

pocket edition

pocketknife

pocket money

pocket park

pocket-sized

pocket veto

pockmark

podcast

poetic justice

poetic license

poet laureate

poetry slam

pogo stick

point-and-click

point-and-shoot

point bar

point-blank

point defect

point-device

pointe shoe

point guard

pointing device

point lace

point man

point of honor

point of no return

point of order

point of sale

point-of-service

point of view

point-shaving

point source

point spread

point system

point woman

pointy-head

poison gas

poison-pen letter

poison pill

poke check

poker face

polar angle

polar axis

polar bear

polar cap

polar circle

polar coordinate

polar front

polar ice cap

polar star

poleax, poleaxe

polestar

pole vault

police action

police court

police dog

police force

policeman

police officer

police power

police procedural

police reporter

police state

police station

policewoman

policyholder

policymaking (policy-)

political action committee

political economy

politically correct

politically incorrect

political prisoner

political science

polka dot

pollen count

poll tax

polo coat

polo shirt

polyvinyl chloride

pommel horse

pompom, pompon

pond scum

pontoon bridge

pony express

ponytail

Ponzi scheme

pooh-pooh

poolroom

poolside

pool table

poop deck

pooper-scooper

poo-poo

poor box

poor boy, po'boy

poor farm

poorhouse

poor law

poormouth

pop art, Pop Art

popcorn

popeyed

pop fly

popgun

popinjay

poppet valve

poppycock

poppy seed

pop tent

pop-top
popular front
porcelain enamel
pork barrel
pork belly
porkpie
pork rind
portal system
portal tomb
portal-to-portal
porterhouse
porthole
port of call
port of entry
port running
positional notation
position paper
position vector
positive law
postage meter
postage stamp
postal card
postal order
postal service
postal system
postbox
postcard, post card

postdate
posterboard
poster boy
poster child
poster color
poster girl
poster paint
postgraduate
posthaste
posthole
postman
postmark
postmaster
postmaster general
postmistress
postmodern
postnasal drip
postnuptial
post office
post office box
post-op, postop
postoperative
postpaid
postproduction
postscript
postseason
posttraumatic

post-truth

postwar

postwoman

potato chip

potato skin

potbelly

potbelly stove

potboil

potboiler

potbound

potboy

pot cheese

potential difference

potential energy

pothead

potholder

pothole

pothook

pothouse

pothunter

pot liquor

potluck

pot metal

pot roast

<u>potsherd</u>, potshard

<u>potshot</u>, pot shot

pot sticker

potstone

potter's clay

potter's field

potter's wheel

potty chair

potty mouth

poulter's measure

pounce box

pouncet box

pound cake

pound-foolish

pound-force

pound key

pound of flesh

pound sign

pound sterling

pour point

poverty level

poverty-stricken

powdered sugar

powder horn

powder keg

powder metallurgy

powder monkey

powder puff *n.*

powder-puff *adj.*

powder room

powerboat	practical joke
power brake	practical nurse
power broker (power)	practice teacher
power chord	prairie schooner
power cycle	praiseworthy
power dive	prayer beads
power drill	prayer book
powerhouse	prayer meeting
power kite	prayer rug
powerlifting	prayer shawl
power mower	prayer wheel
power of appointment	precious metal
power of attorney	precious stone
power pack	preferred stock
power plant	prenuptial agreement
power play	preparatory school
power politics	prepositional phrase
power shovel	presence of mind
power station	present arms
power steering	press agency
power strip	press agent
power structure	press association
power takeoff	pressboard
power train	press box
power trip	press conference
power walking	press gang, pressgang *n.*
powwow	press-gang *tr.v.*

press kit

pressman

pressmark

press of sail

press release

pressroom

press run, pressrun

press secretary

presstime

pressure cabin

pressure-cook

pressure cooker

pressure drag

pressure gauge

pressure group

pressure point

pressure suit

presswork

previous question

previous to

price fixing

price index

price point

price support

price tag

price war

pride of place

prima ballerina

prima donna

prima facie

primal scream

primal therapy

primary accent

primary care

primary cell

primary coil

primary color

primary tooth

prime interest rate

prime meridian

prime minister

prime mover

prime number

prime rate

prime time

primordial soup

primrose path

prince charming

prince consort

principal focus

principal parts

print bar

printed circuit

printed matter

printer's devil
printhead
printing office
printing press
printmaking
printout
print spooler
print wheel
prior restraint
prior to
prison camp
prisoner of war
prison fever
private detective
private eye
private first class
private parts
private school
private sector
prizefight
prize ring
prizewinner
prizewinning
probable cause
probable error
probate court
probation officer

process printing
producer gas
producer goods
producer price index
production line
production well
product placement
profit and loss
profit center
profit sharing
profit taking
program director
programmed instruction
programming language
program music
program trading
progressive education
projection booth
promenade deck
promissory note
promptbook
proof of the pudding
proofread
proof sheet
proof spirit
propellerhead
proper fraction

proper noun

property tax

proprietary colony

prose poem

pro shop

proton synchrotron

proud flesh

proud-hearted

proving ground

provost court

provost guard

provost marshal

pruning hook

pseudo-event

pub-crawl

public-address system

public assistance

public defender

public domain

public eye

public figure

public health

public house

public housing

public key

public law

public library

public offering

public policy

public prosecutor

public relations

public sale

public school

public sector

public servant

public service

public-spirited

public utility

public works

puddingstone

puffed-up

puff pastry

pugil stick

pug nose

pull ahead

pullback

pull date

pull-down menu (pull)

pullout

pullover

pull-tab

pull-up

pulpwood

pumped storage

pumpkinseed

pump-priming (pump)

punchball

punchboard

punch bowl

punch card

punch-drunk

punching bag

punch line

punch-out

punch press

punch tape

punch-up

punctuation mark

punitive damages

punji stick

punk rock

punk rocker

puppy love

puppy mill

pup tent

purchasing power

pureblood

purebred

pure democracy

purl stitch

purple state

purse strings (purse)

pursuit plane

pushback

pushball

push broom

pushbutton

pushcart

pushover

pushpin

push poll

push-pull

pushrod, push rod

pushup, push-up

pussyfoot

pussy-whipped

putlog

putoff

put-on

putout

putting green

putt-putt, put-put

putty knife

put-up

pyramid scheme

Q

quad bike

quadratic equation
quadratic formula
quadruple witching hour
quakeproof
Quaker gun
quaking bog
quality assurance
quality control
quality time
quantum bit
quantum field theory
quantum jump
quantum leap
quantum mechanics
quantum number
quantum physics
quantum state
quantum theory
quark matter
quark number
quark star
quarterback
quarterback sneak
quarter day
quarterdeck
quarterfinal
quarter-hour (quarter)

quartermaster
quarter note
quarter-phase
quarterpipe
quarter rest
quartersaw
quarter section
quarterstaff
quartertone
quartz crystal
quartz glass
quartz lamp
quayside
queen consort
queen mother
queen post
queen regnant
queenside
queen-size
queen truss
queer theory
question mark
quick-and-dirty
quick assets
quick bread
quick fix
quick-freeze

quick kick
quicksand
quickset
quicksilver
quickstep
quick study
quick-tempered
quick time
quick-witted
quid pro quo
quiet title
quitclaim
quizmaster
quiz show
quotation mark

R

rabbit ears
rabbit food
rabbit hole
rabbit punch
rabble-rouser
race-bait, racebait
racecar
racecourse
racehorse
racetrack

racewalking
raceway
racial profiling
racing form
racing skate
rack and pinion
rack railway
rack-rent
racquetball
radar astronomy
radar beacon
radar gun
radarscope
radar telescope
radial engine
radial symmetry
radial tire
radial velocity
radiant energy
radiant flux
radiation pressure
radiation sickness
radiation therapy
radical expression
radical sign
radioactive decay
radioactive series

radio astronomy
radio beacon
radio beam
radiobroadcast
radiocarbon dating
radio collar
radio compass
radio frequency
radio galaxy
radiometric dating
radiophone
radiophoto
radiophotograph
radio spectrum
radiotelegraph
radiotelephone
radio telescope
radio wave
radius vector
rag-and-bone man
ragbag
rag doll *n.*
rag-doll *v.*
raghead
ragman
ragpicker
ragtag

ragtag and bobtail
ragtime
ragtop
rag trade
railbird
railcar
rail fence
rail gun
railhead
railroad
railroad flat
railroading
railroad tie
rail-splitter
railway
rainbow
rain check
raincoat
rain date
raindrop
rainfall
rainfed
rainforest, rain forest
<u>rain gauge</u>, rain gage
rainmaker
rainmaking
rainout

rain shadow

rainspout

rainsquall

rainstorm

rain-wash

rainwater

rainwear

rainy day

rakehell

rake-off

ramrod

ranch dressing

ranch house

random-access memory

random coil

random variable

ransomware

random walk

range finder, rangefinder

rangeland

rank and file

rape shield law

rapid chess

rapid eye movement

rapid-fire

rapid transit

rap session

rap sheet

rare earth

rare-earth element

raree show

rare gas

rareripe

rashguard (rash)

rat cheese

ratemaking

rate of exchange

ratepayer

ratfink

rather than

rat race

rat's next

rat-tail, rattail

rattlebrained

rattlesnake flag

rattletrap

rattrap

rave-up

raw bar

rawboned

raw foodist

raw material

raw sienna

raw silk

ray gun

razorblade, razor blade

razor bump

razor wire

razzle-dazzle

reaction engine

reaction formation

reaction time

reactive thrust

reactor core

reactor vessel

reading desk

reading frame

read-only memory

readout, read-out

ready-made, readymade

ready-mix

ready-to-wear

real estate

reality check

reality principle

real-life

real number

real time

rear admiral

rear end *n.*

rear-end *tr.v.*

rear guard *n.*

rear-guard *adj.*

rearmost

rearview mirror

rear-wheel drive

rebel yell

receiving blanket

receiving end

receiving line

recess appointment

reciprocal pronoun

reciprocating engine

recovered memory

recovery room

recreational vehicle

recreation room

rec room

recumbent bicycle

recurrent fever

recurring decimal

recurve bow

red alert

redbait

red blood cell

red-blooded

redbrick

redcap

red card
red carpet
red cell
red cent
redcoat
red corpuscle
red-dog
red dwarf
redeye
redeye gravy
red-faced
red flag
red giant
red-handed
redhead
redheaded (red-)
red heat
red herring
red-hot
red ink
red lead
red-letter
red light
red-light district
redline
red meat
redneck

red ocher
redout
red-pencil
red ribbon
red shift
redshirt
redskin
red state
red supergiant
red tape
reducing agent
redware
red zone
reedman
reed organ
reed pipe
reed stop
reef knot
reel-to-reel
reentry vehicle
reference book
reference frame
referred pain
reflecting telescope
reflection nebula
reflex angle
reflex arc

reflex camera

reflex hammer

reform school

refracting telescope

refried beans

registered nurse

regius professor

regulator gene

Reign of Terror

reinforced concrete

rejection slip

relapsing fever

relative clause

relative density

relative frequency

relative humidity

relative pitch

relative pronoun

relaxation time

relay race

releasing factor

relief map

relief pitcher

remote control

remote sensing

Renaissance man

Renaissance woman

rent-a-car

rent boy

rent control

rent-free

rent-roll

rent strike

repairman

repairwoman

repeating firearm

repertory company

repetitive strain injury

report card

reproductive cloning

repurchase agreement

reserve bank

reserve clause

reserve currency

reserve price

resistance factor

resistance welding

resonant circuit

rest area

rest energy

rest home

resting cell

restless legs syndrome

restraining order

restraint of trade

retained earnings

retained object

retaining wall

retrieval engine

revealed religion

revenue bond

revenue stamp

revenue tariff

reverberatory furnace

reverse acquisition

reverse appliqué

reverse discrimination

reverse dive

reverse engineering

reverse fault

reverse layup

reverse mortgage

reverse takeover

revolving credit

revolving door

revolving fund

rhetorical question

rheumatic fever

rheumatic heart disease

rheumatoid arthritis

rheumatoid factor

rhyme royal

rhyme scheme

rhyming slang

rhythm and blues

rhythmic gymnastics

rhythm method

ribbed vault

rib-tickling

rib vault

rice paper

rice pudding

rice rocket

rickrack

ridesharing

ride shotgun

ridgeboard

ridgepole

ridge rib

riding habit

riffraff

rifleman

riflescope

rift valley

rift zone

right angle

right ascension

right brain

right-brained

right circular cone

right-click

right face

right field

right fielder

right-hand

right-handed

right-hander

right-hand rule

right-minded

rightmost

right of asylum

right of search

right of way, right-of-way

right-on

right-out

right-side up

rightsize

right stuff

right to choose

right to die

right to know (-to-)

right-to-life

right-to-work law

right wing

rigor mortis

ringback

ringbolt

ring finger

ringfort

ring knocker

ringleader

Ring nebula

Ring of Fire

ringside

ringtone

ringtoss

rinky-dink

riparian rights

ripcord

rip current

rip entry

rip-off

ripple effect

ripple tank

riprap

rip-roaring

ripsaw

ripsnorter

rip tide

rising action

rising rhythm

risk capital

risk factor

rite of passage

ritual murder

riverbank

river basin

riverbed

riverboat

riverfront

riverhead

riverside

roach clip

road agent

roadbed

roadblock

road hog

roadhouse

roadkill

road map

road metal

road race

road rage

road show

roadside

roadstead

road test

road trip

road warrior

roadway

roadwork

roadworthy

robber baron

robocall

robot bomb

robot pilot

rock-a-bye, rockabye

rock-and-roll ('n')

rock and rye

rock art

rockaway

rock bottom

rockbound, rock-bound

rock candy

rock climbing

rock crystal

rocker arm

rocker cam

rocker panel

rocket docket

rocket engine

rocket plane

rocket science

rocket scientist

rocket ship

rocket sled

rockface

rockfall

rock flour

rock garden

rock hound

rocking chair

rocking horse

rock music

rock 'n' roll

rock oil

rock-ribbed

rock salt

rockshaft

rockslide

rock steady

rock wool

rodman

roentgen ray

rogues' gallery

rogue wave

role model

role-play

role player

role-playing

role-playing game

rollaway

rollback

roll bar

roll call

roller bearing

Rollerblade

roller coaster, rollercoaster

roller hockey

roller skate

roll film

rolling blackout

rolling mill

rolling paper

rolling pin

rolling stock

roll-on

rollout

rollover

roll-top desk, rolltop desk

roll-up

rollway

Roman nose

rood beam

rood loft

rood screen

roof garden

rooftop

rooftree

room and board

rooming house

roommate

room temperature

roorback

rooster tail *n.*

rooster-tail *intr.v.*

root beer

root canal

root cellar

root crop

root hair

roothold

rootkit

root mean square

rootstock

root system

rope-a-dope

rope tow

ropewalk

rose-colored

rose fever

rose quartz

rose water

rose window

rotary engine

rotary harrow

rotary joint

rotary plow

rotary press

rotary tiller

rotary-wing craft

rotator cuff

rotgut

rotten borough

rottenstone

rough-and-ready

rough-and-tumble

rough breathing

roughcast

rough cut

roughdry

roughhouse

roughneck

roughrider

roundabout

round dance

round hand

round-heeled

roundhouse

round-off

round robin

round-shouldered

roundsman

round steak

roundtable

round-the-clock

round trip

roundup

roustabout

rowboat

row house

rowlock

royal blue

royal flush

royal jelly

royal purple

royal we

rubber band

rubber-base paint

rubber cement

rubber check

rubberneck

rubbernecker

rubber stamp *n.*

rubber-stamp *tr.v.*

rubbing alcohol

rubblework

rubdown

ruboff, rub-off

rubout

ruby laser

rucksack

ruck up

rudderpost

rudderstock

rude awakening

ruled surface

rule of engagement

rule of the road

rule of thumb

rumble seat

rumble strip

rummage sale

rumormonger

rumpus room

rumrunner

rum shop

runabout

runaround

runaway

runback

run batted in

runcible spoon

rundown

runaround

runaway

runaway-bride

run-in

runner-up
running back
running board
running dog
running gear
running hand
running knot
running light
running mate
running noose
running start
running stitch
runoff
run-of-the-mill
run-on
run-on sentence
runout
run-through
run-up, runup
runway
rural free delivery
rural route
rush candle
rush hour
rushlight
Russian roulette
Rust belt, rust belt

rustproof
rye bread

S

sabbatical year
saber rattling
saber saw
sack-back dress
sackcloth
sack race
sacred cow
sacrifice bunt
sacrifice fly
saddlebag
saddle blanket
saddlebow
saddlecloth
saddle horse
saddle roof
saddle shoe
saddle soap
saddle sore
saddle stitch
sad sack
safari jacket
safe-conduct
safecracker

safe-deposit box

safeguard

safe house

safekeeping

safelight

safe sex

safety belt

safety circuit

safety glass

safety island

safety kick

safety lamp

safetyman

safety match

safety net

safety orange

safety pin

safety razor

safety valve

saga novel

sagittal plane

sailboard

sailboarding

sailboat

sailcloth

sailplane

Saint Elmos's fire

salad bar

salad days

salad dressing

sale and leaseback

sale-leaseback

sales check

salesclerk

saleslady

salesman

salesperson

salesroom

sales tax

saleswoman

Salisbury steak

salivary gland

Salk vaccine

salsa verde

sal soda

salt-and-pepper

saltbox

saltcellar

salt dome

salt hay

salt lick

salt marsh

salt pan

salt pork

saltshaker

saltwater, salt-water

saltworks

Sam Browne belt

same-sex

sam hill, Sam Hill

sample space

sampling distribution

sampling gate

sandbag

sandbank

sandbar

sandblast

sand-blind

sandboard

sandbox

sand-cast

sand crack

sand dollar

sandhog

sandlot

sandman

sand painting

sandpaper

sandpit

sandstone

sandstorm

sand table

sand trap

sandwich board

sandwich generation

sandwich man

sanitary landfill

sanitary napkin

satellite dish

satellite radio

satin stitch

satin weave

saturated fat

saturation point

Saturday night special

sauceboat

saucebox

saucepan

saucepot

savant syndrome

save-all

saving clause

saving grace

savings account

savings and loan

savings bank

savings bond

savings clause

sawbones

sawbuck

sawdust

sawed-off

sawhorse

saw log

sawmill

saw set

saw-toothed

saxhorn

saxtuba

say-so

scalp lock

scandal sheet

scapegoat

scapegrace

scarecrow

scaredy-cat (scaredy)

scaremonger

scare quotes

scarlet fever

scar tissue

scatterbrain

scatter diagram

scattergood

scattergun

scattering layer

scatter pin

scatterplot

scatter rug

scattershot

scatter-site

scavenger hunt

scene-stealer

scenthound

scheduled caste

schlockmeister

school age

school bag, schoolbag

school board

schoolbook

schoolboy

school bus

schoolchild, school child

school choice

school day

school district

schoolfellow

school figure

schoolgirl

schoolhouse

schoolman

schoolmarm

schoolmaster

schoolmate

schoolmistress

school of thought

schoolroom

schoolteacher

schoolwork

schoolyard

school year

science fiction

scientific creationism

scientific method

scientific name

scientific notation

scissors hold

scissors kick, (scissor)

scoreboard

scorecard

scorekeeper

Scotch egg

Scotch verdict

Scotch woodcock

scoutmaster

scrambled eggs

scramjet

scrapbook

scraperboard

scrapheap, scrap heap

scratchboard

scratch card

scratch hit

scratch line

scratch pad

scratchproof

scratch sheet

scratch test

scratch ticket

screaming meemies

screen burn

screencap

screen dump

screenland

screen memory

screen pass

screenplay

screenprint

screenprinting

screen saver

screenshot

screen test

screen time

screenwriter

screwball

screw cap

screwdriver

screw eye

screw jack

screw propeller

screw thread

screwup, screw-up

scrip issue

scripting language

script kiddie

scriptwriter

scroll saw

scrollwork

scrubland

scrub nurse

scrub suit

scrubwoman

scuba diving

scuff mark, scuffmark

scumbag

scuttlebutt

scuzzball

scuzzbucket

sea anchor

seabed

sea biscuit

seaboard

seaborne

sea bread

sea breeze

sea captain

sea change

sea chest

seacoast

sea dog

sea duty

seafarer

seafaring

sea floor, seafloor

sea-floor spreading

seafood

seafowl

seafront

seagirt

sea glass

seagoing

sea grant college

sea green

seakeeping

sea king

sea-lane

sea legs

sea level

sealift

sealing wax

seal ring

sealskin
sea-maiden, sea-maid
seaman
seaman apprentice
seaman recruit
seamark
sea mile
seamount
seaplane
seaport
sea power
seaquake
search engine
searchlight
search warrant
sea room
sea rover
sea salt
seascape
sea serpent
seashell
seashore
seasickness
seaside
season ticket
seastrand
seatback, seat back

seat belt
seating area
seatmate
seat-of-the-pants
seatrain
seatwork
seawall, sea wall
seawater
seaway
seaworthy
secondary accent
secondary battery
secondary cell
secondary color
secondary consumer
secondary market
secondary offering
secondary school
secondary stress
secondary succession
secondary tissue
second banana
second base
second baseman
second best
second blessing
second childhood

second class *n.*

second-class *adj.*

second cousin

second-degree burn

second fiddle

second-generation

second growth

second-guess

secondhand *adj.*

second hand *n. clock*

second hand *n. source*

secondhand smoke

second home

second line *n.*

second-line *adj.*

second mortgage

second nature

second person

second-rate

second sight

second-story man

second-strike

second string

second thought

second wind

secretary-general

secret ballot

secret key

secret key cryptography

secret partner

secret police

secret service

secret society

secular humanism

security blanket

security guard

seed ball

seedbed

seed cake

seed coat

seedeater

seed money

seed pearl

seed plant

seedpod

seed stock

seedtime

seeing-eye dog

seek time

seersucker

seesaw

see-through

segmental arch

seizure disorder

212

selective service
selectman
selectwoman
self-absorbed
self-addressed
self-adhesive
self-aggrandizement
self-analysis
self-annihilation
self-appointed
self-asserting
self-assertion
self-assured
self-aware
self-basting
self-centered
sclf-cleaning
self-concern
self-confidence
self-conscious
self-contained
self-content
self-control
self-critical
self-defeating
self-defense
self-denial

self-destruction
self-discipline
self-discovery
self-doubt
self-educated
self-employed
self-esteem
self-evident
self-explanatory
self-expression
self-governing
self-gratification
self-help
self-identity
self-image
self-impose
self-improvement
self-indulgence
self-inflict
self-interest
self-justification
self-loading
self-love
self-mastery
self-motivation
self-pity
self-portrait

self-preservation

self-propelled

self-published

self-reliance

self-reproach

self-respect

self-restraint

self-sacrifice

selfsame

self-satisfaction

self-sealing

self-serving

self-starter

self-storage

self-study

self-sufficient

self-taught

self-worth

sellback

sell-by date

seller's market (sellers')

selling climax

selling point

selloff

sellout

sellthrough

semiheavy water

semiprecious stone

senatorial courtesy

senatorial district

senile dementia

senior airman

senior chief petty officer

senior citizen

senior high school

senior master sergeant

senior moment

sense datum

sense organ

sense perception

sensible horizon

sensitivity training

sensory deprivation

sentence adverb

sentence fragment

sentence stress

sentry box

separate school

separation anxiety

septic shock

septic sore throat

septic tank

sergeant at arms

sergeant first class

sergeant major

serial number

series circuit

series-wound

serum sickness

service break

service cap

service ceiling

service charge

service dog

service line

serviceman

service mark

serviceperson

service road

service station

service stripe

servicewoman

set-aside

setback *n. change*

set back *n. football*

set-in

setline

setoff

setout

set piece

set point

setscrew

set theory

setup

setup pitcher

seven seas, Seven Seas

seventh heaven

seventh-inning stretch

severalfold

severance pay

severance tax

sewing circle

sewing machine

sex change surgery

sex hormone

sex kitten

sex object

sex offender

sex offence

sexpot

sex ratio

sex shop

sex slave

sex symbol

sex therapy

sex tour

sex toy

sexual abuse

sexual assault

sexual harassment

sexual intercourse

sexual orientation

sexual relations

sexual selection

shadowbox *intr.v.*

shadow box *n.*

shadow dance

shadow play

shaggy-dog story

shakedown

shaken baby syndrome

shakeout

shakeup

shaking palsy

shale oil

shamefaced

shankpiece

shantytown

shape-note singing

shapeup, shape-up

shapewear

sharecrop

sharecropper

shareholder

shareowner

shareware

sharkskin

sharp-eyed

sharp-nosed

sharpshooter

sharpshooting

sharp-sighted

sharp-tongued

sharp-witted

shatter cone

shatterproof

shatterproof glass

Shawnee cake

shear force

shear strain

shear stress

shearwater

shear wave

sheath knife

shed dormer

she-devil

shedrow

sheep dip, sheep-dip

sheepdog, sheep dog

sheepfold

sheepherder

sheep's eyes

sheepshank
sheepshearing
sheepskin
sheet anchor
sheet bend
sheet glass
sheet lightning
sheet metal
sheet music
shelf cloud
shelf ice
shelf life
shellback
shellfire
shellfish
shellfishery
shell game
shell jacket
shell pink
shellproof
shell shock
shell-shocked (shell)
shelterbelt
shelter tent
shepherd dog
shepherd's pie
shield law

shield volcano
shift key
shilly-shally
shinplaster
shin splints, shinsplints
ship biscuit
shipboard
shipbuilding
ship canal
ship fever
ship fitter
shiplap
shipload
shipman
shipmaster
shipmate
ship money
ship of the line
shipping clerk
shipping fever
ship-rigged
shipshape
shipside
ship's papers
shipway
shipwreck
shipwright

shipyard

shire town

shirtdress, shirt-dress

shirtfront

shirtsleeve

shirttail

shirtwaist

shock absorber

shock jock

shockproof

shock radio

shock therapy

shock troops

shock wave

shoebox

shoegazer

shoegazing

shoehorn

shoelace

shoemaker

shoepac, shoepack

shoeshine

shoestring

shoestring catch

shoetree

shoofly

shoofly pie

shoo-in

shook-up

shootaround

shootdown

shoot-'em-up

shooting gallery

shooting iron

shooting star

shooting stick

shootout, shoot-out

shoot-the-chute

shoot-up

shopkeeper

shoplift

shopping bag

shopping center

shopping list

shopping mall

shop steward

shoptalk

shopworn

shore dinner

shorefront

shore leave

shoreline

shore patrol

short bit

shortbread

shortcake

shortchange

short circuit *n.*

short-circuit *v.*

short-circuit current

shortcoming

short covering

shortcut

short-day

short division

shortened form

shortfall

short fuse

short game

shorthair

short-haired

shorthand

short-handed

short haul

shortlist, short-list *n.*

short-list *tr.v.*

short-lived

short order

short-range

short ribs

short sale

short-sell

short-sheet

short shrift

short sight

shortsighted

short-sold

short-spoken

short-staffed

shortstop

short story

short subject

short-tempered

short-term

short-term memory

short ton

short-waisted

shortwave *adj.*

short wave *n.*

short-winded

shot clock

shotgun

shotgun house

shotgun marriage

shot hole

shot on goal

shot put

shot tower

shoulder bag

shoulder belt

shoulder blade

shoulder board

shoulder girdle

shoulder harness

shoulder holster

shoulder knot

shoulder mark

shoulder pad

shoulder patch

shouting distance

shout-out

shovel hat

shovel-nosed

show-and-tell (and)

show bag

show bill

show biz

showboat

showbread, shewbread

show business

showcase

showdown

shower bath

showerhead

showgirl

showgoer

showman

showoff

showpiece

show place, showplace

show room

showstopper

showtime, show time

shrink-wrap

shuffleboard

shunpike

shutdown

shuteye

shut-in

shutoff

shutout

shutterbug

shuttlecock

shuttle diplomacy

shylock

Siamese twin

sibling species

sickbay

sickbed

sick call

sick day

sick headache

sick leave
sickle feather
sicko
sickout
sick pay
sickroom
sidearm *adj.*
side arm *n.*
<u>sideband</u>, side band
sidebar
sideboard
sideburns
sidecar
side chain
side chair
side dish
side-dress
side dressing
side drum
side effect
side-eye
side-glance
sidekick
sidelight
sideline
sideliner
sidelong

sideman
sideout, side-out
sidepiece
sidereal day
sidereal hour
sidereal month
sidereal time
sidereal year
sidesaddle
sideshow
sideslip
sidespin
sidesplitting
sidestep
side-straddle hop
sidestream smokc
sidestroke
sideswipe
sidetrack
sidewalk
sidewalk superintendent
sidewall
sideways
side-wheeler
side-whiskers
sidewinder
sight draft

sight gag
sighthound
sightline, sight line
sight-read
sight rhyme
sightsee
sightseeing
signboard
signet ring
significance level
significant digits
significant other
sign language
sign manual
sign of the cross
signpost
silent auction
silent butler
silent partner
silent treatment
silica gel
silk cotton
silk hat
silk-screen, silkscreen
silk stocking *n.*
silk-stocking *adj.*
silver age

silver bullet
silver certificate
silver cord
silver lining
silver plate *n.*
silver-plate *tr.v.*
silverpoint
silver screen
silversmith
silver spoon
silver standard
silver-tongued
silverware
silverwork
simon-pure
simple interest
simple machine
simple microscope
simple-minded (simple)
simple pendulum
simple sentence
Simple Simon
simple sugar
sin bin
sine die
sing-along
single blind

single bond

single-breasted

single cross

single entry

single file

single-foot

single-hand

single-handed (single)

single-hearted

single-issue

single knot

single-lens reflex

single-minded

single-phase

singles bar

single-sex

single-space

singlestick

singlesticker

single tax

single-track

singlewide

singsong

sinkerball

sinkhole

sinking fund

sin tax

sippy cup

siren song

sissy bar

sister-in-law

sitcom

sit-down

sit-ski

sitting duck

sitting area

sitting room

situation comedy

situation ethics

sit-up

sitz bath

six-pack

sixpence

sixpenny

sixpenny nail

six-shooter

sixteenpenny nail

sixteenth note

sixth sense

sixty-fourth note

skateboard

skate ski

skeleton key

sketchbook

sketchpad

skew arch

skewback

skewbald

skew lines

ski boot

ski cross

skid fin

skid road

skid row

ski jump

ski lift

ski mask

skimboard

skimboarding

skim milk

skimobile

skin-deep

skin diving

skin effect

skin flick

skinflint

skin game

skin graft

skinhead

skinny-dip

skinny jeans

skin patch

skin-pop

skin test

skintight

skip distance

ski plane, skiplane

ski pole

skirt steak

ski run

ski touring

ski tow

skiwear

skull and crossbones

skullcap

skullduggery (skul)

skull session

sky blue

skyboard

skybox

sky burial

skycap

skydive

sky glow, skyglow

sky-high

skyhook, sky-hook

skyjack

sky lantern

skylight
skylighted
skyline
sky marshal
sky pilot
skyrocket
skysail
skyscraper
skysurfing
skywalk
sky wave
skyway
skywriting
slab-sided
slack-baked
slack-key
slackline
slacklining
slack water
slam-bang
slam dancing
slam dunk *n.*
slam-dunk *v.*
slant rhyme
slapdash
slaphappy
slapjack

slap shot
slapstick
slash-and-burn
slate black
slate blue
slaughterhouse
slave driver
slaveholder
slave state
slave trade
sleazebag
sleazeball
sled dog
sledgehammer
sleep apnea
sleep-in
sleeping bag
sleeping car
sleeping pill
sleeping porch
sleeping sickness
sleep-learning
sleepover
sleepwalk
sleepwalking
sleepwear
sleepyhead

sleeve coupling

sleight of hand

sleuthhound

slice bar

slice of life

slide rule

slide tackle (sliding)

slide valve

sliding scale

slimeball

slingback, sling-back

slingshot

slipcase

slipcover

slipdress, slip dress

slipknot

slip-on

slipover

slipped disk

slippery slope

slip ring

slip sheet

slipshod

slipstitch

slipstream

slip-up

slipware

slipway

slit trench

sloe-eyed

sloe gin

sloop of war

sloppy joe, sloppy Joe

slopwork

slot car

slot machine

slot racing

slotting fee

slouch hat

slow burn

slowdown

slow-footed

slow gait

slow infection

slow match

slow-mo

slow motion

slow-pitch, slo-pitch

slowpoke

slow-twitch

slow whistle

slow-witted (slow)

slugabed

slugfest

slugging percentage
sluiceway
slumber party
slumlord
slush fund
slyboots
smack-dab
smackdown
small arm
small ball
small beer
small blind
small-bore
small bowel
small calorie
small cap
small capital
small change
small-claims court
smallclothes
small fry
small hours
small-minded
small potatoes
smallpox
small print
small-scale

small solar system body
small talk
smalltime (small-) *adj.*
small time *n.*
small-town
smart aleck
smart bomb
smart card
smart drink
smart drug
smart money
smartphone
smart set
smart terminal
smarty-pants
smashmouth
smashup
smelling salts
smoke bomb
smoke detector
smoke-filled room
smokehouse
smokejumper
smokeless powder
smokeless tobacco
smoker's cough
smoke screen (smoke)

smokestack	snakestone
smoking car	snap back
smoking gun	snap-brim
smoking jacket	snap roll
smoking room *n.*	snapshoot
smoking-room *adj.*	snapshot *n. photo*
smoky quartz	snap shot *n. hockey*
smoothbore, smooth bore	snare drum
smooth breathing	sneak preview
smooth muscle	sneak thief
smooth-tongued	sneezeguard
smudge pot	snickerdoodle
smudge stick	sniffer dog
smurf attack	snipe hunt
snack bar	snob appeal
snaggletooth	snollygoster
snail mail	snowball
snail-paced	snowbank
snakebit, snakebitten	snowbike
snakebite	snow blindness
snake charmer	snowblink
snake dance	snowblower (snow)
snake eyes	snowboard
snake in the grass	snowboard cross
snake oil	snowbound
snake pit	snowcap
snakeskin	snowclone

snow cone
snow cover
snowdrift
snowfall
snow fence
snowfield
snowflake
snow job
snowkiting (snow)
snow line
snowmachine
snowmaker
snowmaking
snowman
snowmelt
snowmobile
snowpack
snow park
snow pellet
snowplow
snowshoe
snowskate
snowslide
snowstorm
snowsuit
snow thrower
snow tire

snow-white
snub-nosed
snuffbox
snuff film
soapbox
soap bubble
soap opera
soapstone
soapsuds
sobersided
sobersides
sob sister
sob story
so-called
soccerball
soccer mom
social climber
social contract
social disease
social distancing
social drinker
social insurance
socialized medicine
social justice
social networking
social promotion
social register

social secretary
social studies
social work
social worker
socket wrench
sock puppet
soda ash
soda biscuit
soda bread
soda cracker
soda fountain
soda jerk
soda pop
soda water
sodbuster
soever
sofa bed
so far as
softball
soft-boil
soft-boiled
softbound
soft coal
softcore, soft-core
soft corn
softcover
soft drink

soft drug
soft goods
soft hail
softhead
softheaded
softhearted
soft kill *n.*
soft-kill *v.*
soft-land
soft landing
soft launch
soft line
soft money
soft news
soft paste, soft-paste
soft pedal *n.*
soft-pedal *tr.v.*
softphone
soft release
soft rock
softscape
soft sculpture
soft sell
soft serve
soft-shoe
soft shoulder
soft soap *n.*

soft-soap *tr.v.*

soft-spoken

soft spot

soft-top

soft touch

software

soft water

softwood

soil pipe

solar battery

solar cell

solar collector

solar constant

solar day

solar filament

solar flare

solar furnace

solar house

solar month

solar nebula

solar panel

solar sail

solar time

solar wind

solar year

soldering iron

soldier of fortune

soldiers' home

sold-out

soleplate

soleprint

solicitor general

solid propellant

solid solution

solid-state

solid-state drive

solid-state physics

solitary confinement

so long

so long as

somebody

someday

somehow

someone

someplace

something

sometime

sometimes

someway

somewhat

somewhere

somewheres

sonata form

song and dance

songsmith

songwriter

sonic barrier

sonic boom

son-in-law

sonnet cycle

sonnet sequence

son of a gun

soothfast

soothsay

soothsayer

soothsaying

soprano clef

sorehead

sore throat

sought-after

soul brother

soul food

soul kiss

soulmate, soul mate

soul music

soul patch

soul-searching

soul sister

sound-alike

sound-and-light show

sound barrier

sound bite, soundbite

sound board *n. panel*

soundboard *n. bites*

sound box

sound card

sound effect

sound hole

sounding board

sounding lead

sounding line

sounding rocket

soundman

sound pollution

sound post

sound pressure

soundproof

sound ranging

soundscape

sound stage, soundstage

soundtrack, sound track

sound truck

sound wave

soup kitchen

soupspoon

sourball

source book

source code

source language

sour cream

sourdough

sour grapes

sour mash

sour orange

sourpuss

sour salt

southbound

southeaster

southern lights

southland

southpaw

southwester

sowbelly

soymilk

soy sauce

space bar

space biology

spaceborne

space cadet

space capsule

space charge

spacecraft

spaced-out

space elevator

space flight

space heater

space medicine

space opera

spaceport

space probe

space science

spaceship, space ship

space shuttle

space sickness

space station

space suit

space-time

space walk

space writer

spadework

spaghetti Western

spareribs

spare tire

spark arrester

spark chamber

spark coil

spark gap

spark generator

sparking plug

sparkling water

sparkling wine

sparkplug *tr.v.*

spark plug *n.*

spark transmitter

spar varnish

speakeasy

speakerphone

speaking in tongues

speaking tube

speak-out

spear-carrier

spear gun

spearhead

spearman

spear phishing

special court-martial

special delivery

special education

special effect

special forces

special interest

special legislation

special-needs (special)

spectral line

speech act

speech community

speechmaker

speechwriter

speedball

speedboat

speedboating

speed brake

speed bump

speed chess

speed dating

speed dial

speed limit

speed metal

speed-read

speed-reading

speed shop

speed skate

speed skating

speed trap

speedup

speedway

speedwriting

spellbind

spellbinder

spellbound

spell checker (spell)

spelldown

spelling bee

spending money

spendthrift

sphere of influence

sphinx-like
spic-and-span (spick-)
spiderhole
spider vein
spike heel
spillover
spillway
spinal column
spin casting
spin doctor
spindrift
spine-chilling
spin fishing
spinning frame
spinning jenny
spinning wheel
spinoff, spin-off
spinout
spin-the-bottle
spin wave
spiral binding
spiral galaxy
spirit lamp
spirit level
spirit of turpentine
spirit of wine
spiritual bouquet

spit and polish
spitball
spit curl
spitfire
spitting image
spit valve
splashboard
splashdown
splashguard
splayfoot
splinter group
split-brain
split decision
split end
split-fingered fastball
split infinitive
split-level
split personality
split rail
split second
split shift
split ticket
spoilsport
spoils system
spoken-word
spokeshave
spokeman

spokesmodel

spokesperson

spokeswoman

sponge bath

sponge cake

sponge rubber

spoon bread (spoon)

spoon-feed

sport coat

sport fish

sportfisherman

sportfishing

sporting chance

sport jacket

sport kite

sports bra

sports car

sportscast

sports coat

sportsman

sports medicine

sportswear

sportswoman

sportswriter

sport utility vehicle

spot check

spotlight

spot-on

spot pass

spot price

spotted fever

spot welding

spray paint

spray skirt

spread eagle *n.*

spread-eagle *adj.*

spreadsheet

spread spectrum

spree killer

springboard

spring chicken

spring-cleaning

spring fever

springform pan

springhead

spring-loaded

spring lock

spring roll

springtide *n. season*

spring tide *n. tides*

springtime

springwood

sprinkler system

spritz bottle

sprocket wheel
sprung rhythm
spun glass
spun silk
spun sugar
spun yarn
spur gear
spur-of-the-moment
spur track
spyglass
spymaster
spyware
squad car
squad goal
squad room
squall line
square bracket
square dance
square knot
square meal
square measure
square one
squared away
square root
square shooter
squawk box
squaw man

squeaky-clean
squeezebox
squeeze play
squib kick
squint-eyed
squirt gun
stability ball
stabilizer bar
stacked heel
stackup
staff of life
staff sergeant
stagecoach
stagecraft
stage fright
stagehand
stage left
stage-manage
stage right
stage-struck
stage whisper
staging area
stained glass
stainless steel
staircase
stair climber (stair-)
stairstep

stair stepper

stairway

stairwell

stakeholder

stakeout

stalk-eyed

stalking-horse

stall-feed

stamping ground

stamp mill

standalone

standard-bearer

standardbred

standard candle

standard deviation

standard error

standard gauge

standard model

standard of living

standard pressure

standard temperature

standard time

standby

stand-down, standdown

standing army

standing crop

standing order

standing room

standing wave

standoff

standoffish

standout

standpat

standpipe

standpoint

standstill

standup, stand-up

starboard

starburst

star-chamber

starch syrup

star-crossed

stardust

star facet

stargaze

stargazer

star key

stark-naked

starlight

starlit

starquake

starry-eyed

star sapphire

starship

starstruck, star-struck
starting block
starting gate
starting line
startup, start-up
statecraft
statehouse, state house
state of the art
stateroom
stateside
statesman
stateswoman
static electricity
stationary bicycle
station break
station house (station)
stationmaster
station wagon
status quo
status symbol
statute law
statute mile
statute of limitations
statutory offense
statutory rape
stave wall
stay-at-home

staying power
stay-in strike
steadfast, stedfast
steak house, steakhouse
steak knife
steam bath
steam beer
steamboat
steam boiler
steam chest
steam engine
steamer rug
steamer trunk
steamfitter
steam heating
steam iron
steampunk
steamroller
steamship
steam shovel
steam table
steam turbine
steel band
steel drum
steel engraving
steel guitar
steel pan

steel-trap
steel wool
steelwork
steelyard
steeplechase
steeplejack
steerageway
steering committee
steering gear
steering wheel
steersman
stellar wind
stem cell
stem christie
stem turn
stemware
stem-winder
stem-winding
step aerobics
stepbrother
stepchild
step dance
stepdaughter
step-down
stepfamily
stepfather
step-in

stepladder
stepmother
stepparent
stepparenting
stepped-up
stepping-off place
steppingstone
step rocket
stepsibling
stepsister
stepson
step stool
step turn
step-up
sterling silver
stern chaser
stern-wheeler
stick and poke
stickball
sticker price
sticker shock
stick figure
stickhandle
sticking plaster
sticking point
stick-in-the-mud
stickpin

stick shift
stick-to-itiveness
stickup
sticky fingers
sticky-outy
sticky sweet *n.*
sticky-sweet *adj.*
sticky wicket
stiff-arm
stiff-necked
stiff upper lip
stiletto heel
still alarm
stillbirth
stillborn
still hunt
still life
still water
stink bomb
stinkpot
stir-crazy
stir-fry
Stirling engine
stirrup-cup
stirrup iron
stirrup leather
stockade fence

stockbreeding
stockbroker
stock car
stock certificate
stock company
stock dividend
stock exchange
stock footage
stockholder
stocking cap
stocking mask
stocking stuffer
stock-in-trade (in)
stockjobber
stockman
stock market
stock option
stockowner
stockpile
stockpot
stockroom, stock room
stock saddle
stock-still
stocktaking
stockyard
stokehold
stokehole

stomachache

stomach pump

stomping ground

stonecutter

stonefaced

stone-ground

stonehearted

stonemason

stone's throw

stonewall

stoneware

stonewash

stonework

stony-faced

stonyhearted

stool pigeon

stoopball

stop-and-go

stopcock

stopgap

stoplight

stop-loss

stop motion

stop order

stop-out

stopover

stoppage time

stop payment

stop street

stopwatch

stopword

storage battery

storage cell

storage device

store-bought

store-boughten

store cheese

storefront

storehouse

storekeeper

storeowner

storeroom

storewide

stormbound

storm cell

storm center

storm door

storm drain

storm sewer

storm surge

storm trooper

storm window

storyboard

storybook

story line
storyteller
storywriter
stouthearted
stovepipe
stovetop
stowaway
straight-ahead
straight and narrow
straight angle
straight-arm
straight arrow
straightaway
straightedge
straight face
straight flush
straightforward
straight-laced
straight-line
straight man
straight off
straight-out
straight poker
straight razor
straight shooter
straight ticket
straightway

strain gauge
straining beam
straitjacket, straightjacket
strait-laced, straight-laced
strand line, strandline
stranger rape
stranglehold
straphanger
strapwork
strawberry blond (blonde)
strawberry mark
strawboard
straw boss
straw-hat
straw man
straw person
straw vote
strawweight
straw wine
streak plate
streambed
streamline
streamlined
streamside
streetcar
street cred
street hockey

streetlight

street luge

street name

streetscape

street-smart

street smarts

street theater

streetwalker

streetwise

strep throat

stressed-out

stress fracture

stress test

stretcher-bearer

stretch mark

stretch-out

stretch reflex

stretch runner

stride piano

strikebound

strikebreaker

strikeout

strikeover

strike price

strike-slip fault

strike zone

striking price

string bass

stringboard

stringcourse

stringed instrument

string line

string quartet

string theory

string tie

strip-cropping

strip joint

strip mall

strip mine *n.*

strip-mine *v.*

stripped-down

strip poker

strip search, strip-search

striptease

strobe light

stroke play

strong-arm

strongbox

strong breeze

strong force

strong gale

stronghold

strong interaction

strongman

strong-minded
strongpoint
strong room
strong safety
strong side
strong suit
struck jury
strung-out
stub nail
stuccowork
studbook
student lamp
student teacher
student union
stud horse
studio apartment
studio couch
stud poker
studwork
study hall
stuffed shirt
stuffing box
stumblebum
stumbling block
stun gun
stunt kite
stuntman

stuntwoman
stylebook
styptic pencil
subject matter
submachine gun
submarine chaser
submarine sandwich
subsequent to
such and such
suchlike
sucker punch
suck-up
suction cup
suction pump
sudden death
sugar cane, sugarcane
sugarcoat
sugar-cured
sugar daddy
sugarhouse
sugaring off
sugar loaf
sugar of milk
sugarplum
suicide watch
suitcase
suit coat

summary court-martial

summerhouse

summersault

summer school

summer solstice

summer stock

summertime

summing-up

sump pump

sunbaked

sunbath

sunbathe

sunbeam

sunbed

sunblock, sun block

sunbonnet

sunbow

sunburn

sunburst

sun dance

Sunday best

Sunday punch

Sunday school

sun deck

sun disk

sundog

sundown

sundowner

sundowning

sundress

sun-dried, sundried

sunglass

sunglow

sun god

sunk fence

sunlamp, sun lamp

sunless tanner

sunny-side up

sun pillar

sun porch, sunporch

sun protection factor

sunrise

sunroof

sunroom

sunscreen

sunset

sunshade

sunshine

sunshine law

sunshower

sunspot

sunstroke

suntan

sun tea

sunup
superabound
superabundant
super band
super bantamweight
supercell
supercharge
supercluster
supercollider
supercomputer
supercontinent
superduper
superego
super featherweight
superfine
super flyweight
superiority complex
superior planet
super lightweight
supermarket
super middleweight
supermodel
supermom
supernova
superstar
supply chain
supply-side

support group
support hose
support system
sure-fire, surefire
sure-footed, surefooted
sure thing
surety bond
surface-active
surface diving
surface-effect ship
surface mail
surface of revolution
surface structure
surface tension
surface-to-air missile
surface-to-surface missile
surface wave
surf and turf
surfboard
surfboarding
surfboat
surfcasting
surfside
surgeon's knot
surge protector
surplus value
surrogate mother

surround sound

survey course

surveyor's level

suspended animation

suspense account

suspension bridge

suspension point

sustained yield

swaddling clothes

swage block

swagger stick

swagman

swallow-tailed

swallow-tailed coat

swamp boat

swamp fever

swampland

swan dive

swan song

swap meet

swashbuckle

swashbuckler

swash letter

SWAT team

swayback

sway bar

swearword

sweatband

sweatbox

sweat equity

sweat lodge

sweatpants

sweatshirt

sweatshop

sweatsuit, sweat suit

sweat test

sweepback

sweep-second hand

sweepstakes

sweet-and-sour

sweetheart

sweet nothings

sweetshop

sweet spot

sweet talk n.

sweet-talk v.

sweet tooth

swell box

swelled head

sweptback

sweptwing

swiftboating

swimming pool

swimsuit

swimwear
swing-by
swing loan
swingman
swing set
swing shift
swing-wing
swipe card
switchback
switchblade
switchboard
switch hitter
switch knife
switchman
switchover
switchyard
swivel chair
swivel-hipped
swizzle stick
sword bayonet
sword cane
sword dance
sword knot
swordplay
swordsman
swordswoman
swung dash

sympathy strike
symphonic poem
symphony orchestra
synchronized swimming
synchronous motor
system administrator
system operator
systems analysis
systems programming

T

tabby weave
tablecloth
table-hop
tableland
table linen
tablemate
table salt
table saw
tableside
tablespoon
table sugar
table talk
table tennis
tabletop
tableware
table wine

tack hammer

tackle box

tackle football

taffeta weave

tagalong, tag-along

tagboard

tag cloud

tag day

tag end

tag line, tagline

tag question

tag sale

tag team *n.*

tag-team *v.*

tailback

tail beam

tailbone

tailcoat

tail end

tail fin, tailfin

tailgate

tailgate party

tail-heavy

tail lamp

taillight

tailor-made

tailor's chalk

tailpiece

tailpipe

tailrace

tailskid

tailspin

tailstock

tailwind, tail wind

takeaway

take-charge

takedown

take-home pay

take-in

take-no-prisoners

takeoff

takeout, take-out

takeover, take-over

take-up

talcum powder

talebearer

talent scout

talent show

taleteller

talkback

talkfest

talking book

talking drum

talking head

talking point

talking-to

talk radio

talk show

talk therapy

tallboy *n. highboy*

tall boy *n. beer can*

tall oil

tallyho

tallyman

tamperproof

tam-tam

tandem bicycle

tandem trailer

tandoor

tank destroyer

tank suit

tank top

tank town

tank trailer

tanning bed

tap dance

tape cartridge

tape deck

tape drive

tapeline

tape measure

tape-record

tape recorder

tape recording

tap house

tap-off

taproom

tap water

tar baby

target date

target language

tarpaper

tar pit

tarradiddle

tartar sauce

taskbar

task force

taskmaster

taskmistress

taste bud

tastemaker

tattletale

tavern sandwich

tax-deductible

tax-deferred

tax evasion

tax-exempt

tax-free

taxicab

taxi dancer

taxi squad

taxi stand

taxiway

taxman

taxpayer

tax return

tax shelter

tea bag

tea ball

tea biscuit

tea caddy

teacake

teacart

tea ceremony

teacher's pet

teacup

tea dance

tea garden

teahouse

teakettle

team foul

team handball

teammate

team play

team teaching

teamwork

tea party

teapot

teardown

teardrop

tear gas *n.*

tear-gas *tr.v.*

tearjerker

tearoom

tear sheet

tearstain

teary-eyed

tea service

teashop

teaspoon

teatime

tea towel

tea tray

tea wagon

tectonic plate

teddy bear, Teddy bear

tee-ball

teedle board

tee-hee, tehee

teenage

teenager

teenybopper

teeny-weeny

teeoff

teepee

tee shirt

teeterboard

teeter-totter

teething ring

teethridge

teetotal

teetotaler, teetotaller

telephone book

telephone booth

telephone exchange

telephone pole

telephone tag

tell-all

telltale

tenant farmer

tenderfoot

tenderhearted

tender offer

tenfold*

ten-gallon hat

tennis bracelet

tennis elbow

tennis shoe

tenor clef

ten-speed

ten-strike

tent city

tenterhook

tent stitch

tenure-track

termination shock

term insurance

term limit

term of art

term paper

terra cotta (terra) (terra-)

terra firma

terra incognita

terrain park

tertiary care

tertiary color

tesla coil

test ban

test case

test-drive

test match

test paper

test pattern

test pilot

test stand

test tube *n.*

test-tube *adj.*

test-tube baby

tetherball

textbook

text edition

text message

text messaging

textspeak

textual criticism

thanksgiving

thankworthy

thank-you

thataway

theatergoer

theater-in-the-round

theater of the absurd

theirselves

theme park

theme song

themselves

then and there

thenceforth

thenceforward

theory of everything

theory of games

therapy dog

thereabouts

thereafter

thereagainst

thereat

thereby

therefor

therefore

therefrom

therein

thereinafter

thereof

thereon

thereto

theretofore

thereunder

thereunto

thereupon

therewith

therewithal

thickhead

thick milk

thickset

thick-skinned

thick-witted

thigh-high

thimblerig

thingamabob

thingamajig

thing-in-itself
thinking cap
think piece
think tank
thin-shinned
third base
third baseman
third class
third degree
third-degree burn
third dimension
third estate
third eye
third eyelid
third force
thirdhand
third house
third market
third party
third person
third rail
third-rate
third-stream
Third World, third world
thirty-second note
thisaway
thitherto

thoroughbass (thorough)
thorough brace
thoroughbred
thoroughfare
thoroughgoing
thoroughpaced
thought experiment
thought reading
threadbare
three-bagger
three-base hit
three-card monte
three-color
three-decker
three-dimensional
three-gaited
three-legged race
three-mile limit
three-piece
three-ply
three-point landing
three-point line
three-quarter binding
three-ring circus
threesome
three-way
three-wheeler

threshing machine

thrift store

throatlatch

throat singing

throttlehold

through-composed

throughout

throughput

throughway

throwaway

throwback

throw-in

throw pillow

throw rug

throw shade

throw-weight (throw)

thrust fault

thrust stage

thruway, throughway

thumb drive

thumbhole

thumb index

thumbnail

thumbnut

thumb piano

thumbprint

thumbscrew

thumbs-down

thumbs-up

thumbtack

thunderbird

thunderbolt

thunderboomer

thunderclap

thundercloud

thunderhead

thundershower

thundersnow

thunderstorm

thunderstruck

ticker tape

ticket office

ticktack, tic-tac

tick-tack-toe, ticktacktoe

ticktock

ticky-tacky

tic-tac-toe

tidal basin

tidal bulge

tidal flat

tidal force

tidal pool

tidal wave

tiddlywinks

tide chart

tideland

tidemark

tide pool

tiderip

tidewaiter

tidewater

tideway

tieback

tie beam

tiebreaker

tie clasp

tie-dye

tie-in

tie line

tie rod

tier table

tie tack

tiger-eye

tight end

tightfisted

tightlipped, tight-lipped

tightrope

tightwad

tilt hammer

tilting board

tiltyard

timber circle

timber hitch

timberland

timberline

timber right

timberwork

time and a half

time and motion study

time bomb

time capsule

timecard

time clock

time-consuming

time deposit

time draft

timcd-release (time-)

time exposure

time frame, timeframe

time-honored

time immemorial

timekeeper

time-lapse

timeline

time loan

time lock

time machine

time note

time-out, timeout

time out of mind

timepiece

time-release

time reversal

timesaving

timescale

timeserver, time-server

time-share

time-sharing

time sheet

time signature

times sign

time study

time suck

timetable

time-tested

time trial

time warp

timework

timeworn

time zone

timing belt

timing chain

tin can

tinderbox

tin ear

tinfoil, tin foil

tinhorn

tinker's damn (dam)

tin lizzie

tinned goods

tin parachute

tin plate *n.*

tin-plate *tr.v.*

tin-pot

tinsmith

tinted glass

tintype

tinwork

tipcart

tip-in

tip-off *n. information*

tip-off *n. basketball*

tipping point

tipstaff

tiptoe

tiptop

tissue paper

tit for tat

title bar

title card

titleholder

title page

title piece
title race
title sponsor
toadeater
toadstone
to and fro *adv.*
to-and-fro *n.*
toaster oven
toastmaster
toastmistress
tobacco road
toecap
toe crack
toe dance
toehold
toe-in
toe loop
toenail
toe ring
toe shoe
toggle bolt
toggle joint
toggle switch
toilet paper
toilet tissue
toilet training
tollbooth

toll bridge
toll-free
tollgate
tollhouse
tomboy
tombstone
tomcat
tomfool
tomfoolery
Tommy gun
tommyrot
tom-tom
tone arm
tone cluster
tone color
tone-deaf
tone language
tone poem
tone row
tongue and groove
tongue depressor
tongue-in-cheek
tongue-lashing
tongue-tie
tongue-tied
tongue twister
tonic accent

tonic water

tonight

toolbar

toolbox

toolkit

toolmaker

toolshed

toothache

tooth and nail

toothbrush

tooth fairy

toothpaste

toothpick

toothpowder

top banana

top boot

topcoat

top dog

top dollar

top-down

top-drawer

top-dress

top dressing

topflight

top hat

top-heavy

top-hole

topic sentence

topknot

top-level

toplofty

topmost

top-notch, topnotch

topological space

top round

topsail schooner

top-secret

topside

topsider

topsoil

topspin

topstitch

topsy-turvy

torchbearer

torch song

torpedo boat

torpedo tube

torque converter

torsion balance

torsion bar

tosspot

tossup

total eclipse

tote bag

tote board

totem pole

touch-and-go

touchback

touchdown

touch football

touchhole

touchline

touchpad, touch pad

touch-proof

touchscreen, touch screen

touchtone

touch-type

touchup

touchy-feely

tough love

tough-minded

touring car

tourist class

tourist trap

tow bag

towboat

towelhead

tower of silence

towhead

towline

town crier

town hall

townhouse, town house

town manger

town meeting

townscape

townsfolk

townsman

townspeople

townswomen

towpath

tow sack

trace element

trace fossil

tracer bullet

track and field

trackball

track event

tracking shot

tracking station

tracking stock

trackless trolley

track light

trackman

track meet

track record

trackside

tracksuit

trackwalker

trackway

tract house

traction kite

tractor-trailer

trade acceptance

trade book

tradecraft

trade discount

trade edition

trade-in

trade language

trademark

trade name, tradename

tradeoff, trade-off

trade paperback

trade rat

trade route

trade school

trade secret

tradesman

tradesperson

tradeswoman

trade union

trade wind

trading card

trading post

trading stamp

traditional jazz

traffic circle

traffic island

traffic light

tragic flaw

tragic irony

<u>trail bike</u>, trailbike

trailblazer

trailblazing

trailbreaker

trailer park

trailhead

trailing edge

trail mix

trailside

trainband

trainbearer

training school

training table

training wheels

trainload

trainman

train oil

train wreck

tramcar

tramline

tramp stamp

tramp steamer

tramway

transfer payment

transform fault

transistor radio

transition element

transverse arch

transverse dune

transverse flute

transverse process

trap and trace device

trapeze artist

trap gun

trap house

traplight

trapline

trapshooting

trash compactor

trashcan

trash talk *n.*

trash-talk *intr.v.*

travel agency

travel guide

traveler's check

traveling salesman

traveling salesperson

traverse rod

trawl line

trawl net

tray table

treadmill

treasure hunt

treasure-trove

treaty port

treble clef

tree farm

treehouse

tree-hugger

tree line, treeline

tree surgery

treetop

trench coat

trencherman

trench mortar

trendsetter

trestle table

trestlework

trial and error

trial balance

trial balloon

trial jury

trial run

tribesman

tribespeople

tribeswoman

trickle charge

trickle-down

trickle-up

trick or treat *interj.*

trick-or-treat *intr.v.*

tried-and-true

trigger-happy

triggerman

trip-hop

triple agent

triple-decker

triple digits

triple-double

triple figure

triple-header, tripleheader

triple jump

triple measure

triple play

triple point

triple rhyme

triple time

triple-tongue

triple witching hour

trolley bus

trolley car

troopship

trophy wife

tropical cyclone

tropical depression

tropical fish

tropical storm

tropical year

tropicbird

trotline

troublemaker

troubleshoot (trouble-)

troubleshooter (trouble-)

troublesome

troy weight

truant officer

truck cap

truck farm

truckle bed

truckload

truck stop

true believer

true bill

true-blue

trueborn

true-crime

true-false test

truelove

true lovers' knot
truepenny
true rhyme
true rib
trump card
trumped-up
trundle bed
trunk hose
trunk line
trunk show
truss bridge
trustbuster
trust company
trust fund
trust fund baby
trust territory
trustworthy
truth-function
truth serum
truth table
true-value
tryout
trysail
try square
tubeless tire
tube pan
tube sock

tube top
tub-thump
tubular bell
tucker-bag
tuck-point
tuckshop
tugboat
tug of war
tumbledown
tumble-dry
tumbleset
tumbling box
tummy tuck
tumpline
tunesmith
tune-up
tungsten lamp
tungsten steel
tuning fork
tuning head
tuning machine
tuning system
tunnel vault
tunnel vision
turbulent flow
turf accountant
turkey trot

Turkish bath
Turkish delight
Turkish towel
turmeric paper
turnabout
turnaround
turnbuckle
turncoat
turndown
turned-on
turning point
turnkey
turnoff
turn-on
turnout
turnover
turnpike
turn signal
turnspit
turntable
turnup
turtleback
turtleneck
tussie-mussie
tutti-frutti
tut-tut
TV dinner

twelve-step, 12-step
twelve-tone
twenty-one
twenty-twenty, 20/20
twice-laid
twice-told
twilight sleep
twilight zone
twin bed
twin bill
twinborn
twin-engine
twinjet
twin-screw
twinset, twin set
twin-size
twin-tip skis
twist drill
twist tie
two-bagger
two-base hit
two-bit
two bits
two-by-four
two-dimensional
two-edged
two-faced

two-fisted
twofold*
two-handed
two-master
two-phase
two-piece
two-ply
two-seater
two-spirit
two-spot
two-step
two-time
two-tone
two-touch
two-way
two-way mirror
two-wheeler
type bar
typecast
typeface
type-high
type locality
type metal
typescript
typeset
type site
type species

type specimen
typestyle, type style
typewrite
typewriter
typewriting
typographical error

U

ugly duckling
uncalled-for
uncared-for
uncertainty principle
uncovered option
underachieve
underact
underactive
underage
underarm
underbelly
underbid
underbody
underboss
underbred
underbrush
underbuy
undercapitalization
undercapitalize

undercard
undercarriage
undercharge
underclass
underclassman
underclothes
underclothing
undercoat
undercount
undercover
undercurrent
undercut
underdeveloped
underdog
underdone
underdrawers
underdress
undereducated
underemphasize
underemployed
underestimate
underexpose
underfeed
underflow
underfoot
underfund
undergarment

undergird
undergo
undergrad
undergraduate
underground
Underground Railroad
undergrowth
underhand
underhanded
underinsured
underlain
underlay
underlayment
underlet
underlie
underline
underlining
underlying
undermine
undermost
undernourish
underpaid
underpants
underpass
underpay
underperform
underpin

underpinning
underplay
underpriced
underprivileged
underrate
underreport
underrepresented
underscore
undersea
undersecretary
undersell
undersexed
undershirt
undershoot
undershorts
undershot
underside
undersign
undersigned
undersized
underskirt
undersold
understate
understated
understatement
understory
understudy

undersubscribed
undersupply
undersurface
undertake
undertaker
undertaking
under-the-counter
under-the-table
undertone
undertook
undertow
underuse
undervalue
underwater
underway
underwear
underweight
underwent
underwire
underworld
underwrite
underwriter
unearned run
unemployment insurance
uneven bars
unheard-of
unhoped-for

unidentified flying object

unified field theory

union church

union jack

union label

union shop

union suit

union territory

unit cost

unit pricing

universe of discourse

unlawful combatant

unlooked-for

unsportsmanlike

unthought of

up-and-coming

up-and-down

upbeat

up-bow

upbringing

upbuild

upcast

upchuck

up-close

upcoming

upcountry

upcycle

update

updraft

upend

upfront, up-front

upgrade

upgrowth

upheaval

upheave

uphill

uphold

upkeep

upland

uplift

uplink

upload

upmarket

upmost

upper atmosphere

upper bound

uppercase

upper class

upperclassman

upper crust

uppercut

upper hand

uppermost

upraise

upright
upright piano
uprising
upriver
uproot
ups and downs
upset price
upshot
upside
upside down
upside-down cake
upsize
upslope
upspring
upstage
upstairs
upstart
upstate
upstream
upstroke
upsurge
upsweep
upswing
uptake
up-tempo, uptempo
up-the-aisle
uptick

uptight
uptime
up-to-date
up-to-the-minute
uptown
uptrend
upturn
upwardly mobile
upward mobility
upwelling
upwind
urban dance
urban forest
urban legend
user-friendly
username
utility knife
utility program
utility room
utilization review

V

vacation land
vacuum bottle
vacuum casting
vacuum cleaner
vacuum drying

vacuum energy
vacuum flask
vacuum fluctuation
vacuum gauge
vacuum-packed
vacuum pressure
vacuum pump
vacuum tube
vainglory
value-added
value-added tax
valued policy
value judgment
valve-in-head engine
Vandyke beard
Vandyke collar
vanishing point
vanity case
vanity plate
vanity press
vanload
vanpool
vantage point
vapor lock
vapor pressure
vapor trail
vaporware

variable annuity
variable cost
variable logic
variable-rate mortgage
variable resistor
variable star
variety meat
variety show
variety store
vaulting horse
vector graphic
vegetable kingdom
vegetable oil
vegetable wax
veggie burger
vending machine
venetian blind
Venetian glass
venture capital
verbal adjective
verb phrase
vernal equinox
vernal pool
vernier caliper
vernier rocket
vernier scale
vertical angle

vertical circle
vertical file
vested interest
vest-pocket
vestryman
vestrywoman
vicar general
vice admiral
vice-admiralty
vice chancellor
vice consul
vice president (vice-)
vice regent
vice squad
vice versa
vicious circle
victimless crime
video blog
video camera
video card
videocassette
videocassette recorder
videoconference
videodisc
video display
video game
video gaming

video jockey
videophone
videotape
Vienna sausage
viewfinder
viewpoint
viewshed
vigilance committee
vineyard
vineyardist
vintage year
violent storm
virgin olive oil
virgin wool
virtual image
virtual machine
virtual memory
virtual reality
virtuous circle
visible light
visible speech
vision quest
visiting card
visiting fireman
visiting nurse
visiting professor
visiting teacher

visual acuity
visual aid
visual art
visual binary
visual field
visually impaired
vital capacity
vital signs
vital statistics
vitreous enamel
vocal cords
vocal percussion
vocal tic
vocal tract
voice box
voicemail, voice mail
voice-over, voiceover
voice part
voiceprint
voice vote
volatile oil
volcanic arc
volcanic glass
volleyball
voltage divider
volume strain
voluntary muscle

voodoo
vote getter
voting machine
voting stock
vowel fracture
vowel mutation
vulture capitalism

W

waffle iron
waffleweave
wage earner
wage scale
wage slave
wageworker
wagon-lit
wagonload
wagon train
wagon vault
wainwright
waistband
waistcloth
waistcoat
waistline
waist pack
wait-a-bit
wait-a-minute

waiting game
waiting list
waiting room
waitlist
waitperson
wait staff, waitstaff
wakeboard
wake-up call
walkabout
walkaway
walkie-talkie
walk-in
walking bass
walking delegate
walking papers
walking stick
walk-off
walk of life
walk-on
walkout
walkover
walk-through
walkup, walk-up
walkway
walky-talky
wallboard
wall cloud

walleyed
wallflower
wall hanging
wallpaper
wall plate
wall plug
wall rock
wall-to-wall
wallyball
walrus mustache
wanderlust
Wankel engine
war baby
war bonnet
war bride
war chest
war correspondent
war crime
war cry
war dance
ward healer
warding off
ward room
warehouse
wareroom
warfare
warfighter

war game *n.*

war-game *v.*

war hawk

warhead

warhorse, war-horse

warlord

warmblood

warm-blooded

warm boot

warmed-over

warm front

warm fuzzies

warm-hearted

warming pan

warmonger

warm-up, warmup

warning coloration

warning track

war of nerves

war paint

warp and woof

war party

warpath

warplane

warp speed

warrant officer

war room

warship

wartime

war-torn

war zone

wash-and-wear

washbasin

washboard

washbowl

washcloth

washday

wash drawing

washed-out

washed-up

washerman

washerwoman

washing machine

washman

washout

washrag

washroom

wash sale

washstand

washtub

washup

washwoman

wasp waist

wasp-waisted

wastebasket
wasteland
wastepaper
wastepaper basket
waste pipe
waste product
wastewater
wasting asset
watchband
watch cap
watchcase
watchdog
watch fire
watch glass
watchmaker
watchman
watch night
watchtower
watchword
water ballet
waterbed
water biscuit
water blister
waterboard, water board
waterboarding
water boatman
waterborne, water-borne

waterbus
water cannon
water closet
watercolor
water column
water-cool
water cooler
watercourse
watercraft
water cycle
water dog
watered-down
waterfall
waterfinder
waterfront
water gap
water gas
water gate
water gauge
water glass
water gun
water hammer
water hole
water ice
watering can
watering hole
watering place

watering pot

water jacket *n.*

water-jacket *tr.v.*

water key

water level

water line, waterline

waterlogged

water main

waterman

watermark

water mill

water on the brain

water park

water parting

water pill

water pipe

water pistol

water polo

waterpower

waterproof

water-repellent

water-resistant

water right

waterscape

water scooter

watershed

waterside

water ski, waterski

water softener

water-soluble

watersports

waterspout

water sprite

water strider

water supply

water system

water table

water taxi

watertight

water tower

water vapor

waterway

<u>water wheel</u>, waterwheel

water wings

water witch

waterworks

watt-hour

wattle and daub

wattmeter

watt-second

waveband

wave equation

waveform

wavefront

wave function
waveguide
wavelength
wave pool
wave tank
wave train
wave trap
wax museum
wax paper
waxwork
waybill
wayfarer
wayfaring
waylay
way-out
waypoint
ways and means
wayside
way station
wayworn
weak-kneed
weak-minded
weak sauce, *n.*
weak-sauce, *adj.*
weak side
weak sister
wealth effect

wear and tear
weasel word
weather balloon
weather-beaten
weatherboard
weatherboarding
weather-bound
weather bureau
weathercast
weathercock
weather deck
weather eye
weatherglass
weathermaker
weatherman
weather map
weatherproof
weather ship
weather station
weather strip *n.*
weather-strip *tr.v.*
weather stripping
weathervane
weather-wise
weatherworn
weaver's hitch
weaver's knot

webcam
webcast
weblog
webmail
webmaster
web member
webmistress
webpage, Web page
web press
website, Web site
webspinner
websurf
wedding-cake
wedding ring
wedding vase
wedge issue
wedge tomb
weed and feed
weed out
weed whacker
weekday
weekend
weekender
weekend warrior
weeklong
weeknight
weightlifter, weight lifter

weightlifting
weight training
welcome mat
welfare state
welfare work
well-adjusted
well-appointed
well-balanced
well-being
wellborn
well-bred
well-defined
well-disposed
well-done
well-endowed
well-favored
well-fed
well-fixed
well-found
well-founded
well-groomed
well-grounded
well-handled
wellhead
well-heeled
well-intentioned
well-knit

well-known

well-mannered

well-meaning

well-meant

well-nigh

well-off

well-preserved

well-read

well-rounded

well-spoken

wellspring

well-taken

well-thought-of

well-timbered

well-timed

well-to-do

well-turned

well-wisher

well-worn

welterweight

western omelet

wetback

wet bar

wet blanket

wet dream

wetland

wet monsoon

wet nurse *n.*

wet-nurse *tr.v.*

wet pack

wetsuit, wet suit

wetting agent

whaleback

whaleboat

whammy bar

whatchamacallit

whatever

whatnot

whatsoever

wheat beer

wheat bread

wheat germ

wheel and axle

wheelbarrow

wheelbase

wheelchair

wheeler-dealer

wheel horse

wheelhouse

wheel lock

wheelman, wheelsman

wheel window

wheelwork

wheelwright

whenas

whencesoever

whenever

whensoever

whereabouts

whereas

whereat

whereby

wherefore

wherefrom

wherein

whereinto

whereof

whereon

wheresoever

wherethrough

whereto

whereunto

whereupon

wherever

wherewith

wherewithal

whetstone

whey-face

whichever

whichsoever

whipcord

whip hand

whiplash

whippersnapper

whipping boy

whipsaw

whipstall

whipstitch

whirlpool

whirlwind

whirlybird

whiskbroom

whiskey sour

whistleblower (whistle-)

whistle stop *n.*

whistle-stop *intr.v.*

whiteboard

white book

white bread *n.*

white-bread *adj.*

whitecap

white chip

white chocolate

white-collar

whited sepulcher

white elephant

whiteface

white-faced

white feather
white flag
white frost
white gasoline
white-glove
white gold
white goods
white-headed
white heat
white hope
white-hot
white knight
white-knuckle
white lie
white light
white lightening
whitelist
white-livered
white magic
white man's burden
white meat
white metal
white night
white noise
whiteout
white pages
white paper

white pepper
whiteprint
white room
white sale
white sauce
white-shoe
white slave
white slaver
whitesmith
white space
white squall
white supremacist
white tie
white trash
whitewall tire
whitewash
whitewater
whitersoever
whiz-bang, whizz-bang
whiz kid
whodunit, whodunnit
whoever
whole blood
whole cloth
whole gale
wholehearted
whole hog

whole language

whole life insurance

whole milk

whole note

whole number

whole rest

wholesale

wholesome

whole step

whole tone scale

whole-wheat

whomever

whomso

whomsoever

whooping cough

whorehouse

whoremaster

whoremonger

whoreson

whoso

whosoever

wickerwork

wicketkeeper

wide-angle

wide area network

wide-awake

wide-body

wide-eyed

wide-open

wideout

wide-ranging

wide receiver

widescreen

widespread

widow's mite

widow's peak

widow's walk

wifebeater

wiggle room

wigwag

wildcard, wild card

wildcat

wildcatter

wild-eyed

wildfire

wildlife

wild pitch

wildwood

willowware

willpower, will power

willy-nilly

windbag

wind-bell

windblast

windblown
windborne, wind-borne
windbreak
wind-broken
windburn
wind-chill factor
wind chimes
wind cone
windfall
wind farm
windflaw
wind gap
wind harp
winding-sheet
windjammer
windmill
window box
window casing
window-dressing
window envelope
windowpane
window seat
window shade
window-shop
windowsill
windpipe
windproof

windsailing
windscreen
wind shake
wind shear
windshield
windsock
Windsor chair
Windsor knot
Windsor tie
wind sprint
windstorm
windsucking
windsurf
windsurfer
windsurfing
windswept
wind tee
wind tunnel
wind turbine
wind-up, windup
winebibbing
wind cellar
wind cooler
wineglass
winegrower
winemaking
winepress

wineskin

wine steward

wind taster

winetasting

wingback

<u>wing chair</u>, wingchair

wing collar

wingding

wing-footed

wing loading

wingman

wingnut, wing nut

wingover

wingspan

wingspread

<u>wingtip</u>, wing tip

winner's circle

winning gallery

winning opening

winning post

winter-feed

winterkill

winter solstice

wintertime

wintry mix

wiped-out

wipeout

wiredraw

wire fraud

wire gauge

wire glass

wireline

wireman

wirepuller

wire rope

wire service

wiretap

wire-to-wire

wirewalker

wirework

wisdom literature

wisdom tooth

wiseacre

wisecrack

wise guy

wise man

wisenheimer

wise woman

wishbone

wish fulfillment

wishful thinking

wish list

wish-wash

wishy-washy

witchcraft
witch doctor
witches' brew
witches' broom
witch-hunt, witch hunt
witching hour
withdraw
withdrawal
withdrawn
withhold
withholding tax
withindoors
with-it
without
withoutdoors
withstand
witness box
witness stand
wobbleboard
woebegone
wolf whistle
woolly pully
woman about town
woman of letters
woman of the hour
woman of the world
womanpower

woman-to-woman
womenfolk
womankind
women's rights
women's room
women's wear
wonder drug
wonderland
wonderwork
wood alcohol
woodbin
woodblock
woodcarving
woodchipper
woodchopper
wood coal
woodcraft
woodcrafter
woodcut
woodcutter
woodcutting
wood engraving
woodenhead
wooden Indian
wooden nickel
woodenware
woodgrain

woodland	word deafness
woodlot, wood lot	word for word
woodman	word-hoard
woodnote	<u>wordmark</u>, word mark
woodpile	wordmonger
woodprint	word of mouth
wood pulp	word order
woodshed	word painting
wood shot	wordplay
woodsman	word processing
wood tar	word processor
woodturning	word salad
woodwind	wordsmith
woodwork	word square
woodworking	workaday
woolgather	workaround
wool grease	workbag
woolgrower	workbench
woolly-headed	workboat
woolsack	workbook
wool shed	work camp
woolskin	workday
Worcestershire sauce	worker-priest
word association test	workers' compensation
word blindness	work ethic
wordbook	workfare
word cloud	work farm

workflow

work force, workforce

work for hire

work function

work hardening

workhorse

workhouse

working class

working day

working dog

working fluid

working girl

workingman

working memory

working papers

workingwoman

work in progress

workload

workman

workmanlike

workmanship

workmen's compensation

work of art

workout

workpeople

workplace

work release

workroom

worksheet

workshop

work song

workspace

workstation

work stoppage

work study

worktable

work to rule

workup

workweek

workwoman

worldbeat

world-beater

world-class

world line

worldly-wise

world music

world power

world-renowned

world's fair

world-shaking

world soul

worldview

world-weary

worldwide

worm-eaten

worm fence

worm gear

wormhole

worm screw

worm's-eye view

worm wheel

worn-out

worry beads

worrywart

worst-case

worthwhile

would-be

wove paper

wraparound

wrapping paper

wrap-up

wrecking bar

wrest pin

wristband

wristlock

wrist pin

wrist shot

wristwatch

write-down

write-in

write-off

write-protect

writer's block

writer's cramp

write-up

writing paper

writ of election

writ of error

writ or prohibition

writ of summons

wrongdoer

wrongful birth

wrongful death

wrong-headed

wrought iron

<u>wrought-up</u>, wrought up

X

x-radiation

X-rated

<u>x-ray</u>, X-ray

x-ray astronomy

x-ray diffraction

x-ray microscope

x-ray spectrometer

x-ray spectrometry

x-ray spectroscope

x-ray spectroscopy

x-ray therapy
x-ray tube

Y
yacht club
yachtsman
yachtswoman
yackety-yak
yadda yadda yadda
yard bomb
yard goods
yardman
yardmaster
yard of ale
yard sale
yardstick
yearbook
year-end, yearend
yearlong
year-over-year
year-round
yea-sayer
yeast infection
yellow-bellied
yellow card
yellow dog
yellow-dog contract

yellow fever
yellow journalism
yellow pages
yellow peril
yellow sheet
yellowware
yeoman of the guard
yes man
yoo-hoo
YouTuber
Yorkshire pudding
you-all, y'all
you guys
young blood
yourself
yourselves
youth hostel
youthquake
yo-yo
yule log
Yuletide
yuppie flu

Z
zebra crossing
zero auxiliary
zero-base

zero-coupon

zero-day attack

zero-defect

zero gravity

zero hour

zero-point energy

zero population growth

zero-rate

zero-sum game

zero tolerance

zigzag

zigzagger

ZIP Code

zip cuffs

zip gun

<u>zipline</u>, zip-line

ziplock

zodiacal light

zonal soil

zone defense

zone melting

zone of leaching

zonetime

zookeeper

zoological garden

zoom lens

zoot suit

BONUS WORDS

RHYMING

ack-ack
airy-fairy
argy-bargy
aye-aye
blah-blah-blah
boogie-woogie
bonbon
bonton
boo boo
bow-wow
boy toy
buddy-buddy
bye-bye
can can
cha cha
choo-choo
chop-chop
chuck-a-luck
chugalug
claptrap
culture vulture
doo-doo
doom and gloom
dumdum

eeksie-peeksie
faghag
fender-bender
flubdub
fogdog
fuddy-duddy
funny money
gloom and doom
goody-goody
goof proof
goo-goo
green screen
ha-ha
hanky-panky
haw haw
heat-treat
heebie-geebies
helter-skelter
herky-jerky
heyday
higgledy-piggledy
hippy-dippy
hubba-hubba
hubble-bubble
humdrum
hurdy-gurdy
hurly-burly

hurry-scurry

hush-hush

itsy-bitsy

itty-bitty

jeez Louise

loosey-goosey

lose-lose

lovey-dovey

meet and greet

mumbo jumbo

namby-pamby

night-light

night-night

niminy-piminy

nitty-gritty

nitwit

no-go

no-no

okey-dokey

pell-mell

palsy-walsy

pan and scan

peewee

pegleg

pell-mell

phony-baloney

pitter-patter

pooper-scooper

poo-poo

pop-top

pom-pom

pooh-pooh

powwow

putt-putt

ragbag

ragtag

razzle-dazzle

rinky-dinky

rocket docket

rope-a-dope

shoot-the-chute

sinbin

snail mail

sump pump

super-dupers

swing-wing

tam-tam

tee-hee

teeny-weeny

teepee

tie-dye

tiny winey

tom-tom

tramp stamp

tussy-mussie
tutti-frutti
tut-tut
voodoo
walkie-talkie
wear and tear
wheeler-dealer
willy-nilly
wingding
yadda yadda yadda
yoo-hoo
yo-yo
zoot suit

VARYING VOWELS

acey-ducey
chitchat
criss cross
dilly-dally
ding-dong
fiddle-faddle
flimflam
flipflop
heehaw
high-ho
hip-hop
hobnob

hodgepodge
hoity-toity
hootchy-kootchy
hotch-potch
house mouse
hugger-mugger
knick-knack
knickknack
mishmash
pitpat
pitter-patter
rickrack
riffraff
shilly-shally
sing song
teeter-totter
ticktack
tick-tack-toe
ticktock
ticky-tacky
tip top
tit for tat
whipper-snapper
wigwag
wish-wash
wishy-washy
zigzag

STUPID, AWKWARD OR CLUMSY

airhead
bampot
birdbrain
blockhead
bonehead
bubblehead
bullheaded
butthead
chowderhead
chucklehead
clodhopper
deadhead
dimwit
dingbat
ding-dong
dipstick
dumbbell
dumdum
dummkopf
dunderhead
egghead
fathead
featherbrain
goofball
goof-off
half-wit
harebrained
knucklehead
lamebrain
loggerhead
lunkhead
meathead
muddleheaded
numbskull
pinhead
rattleheaded
scatterbrain
stumblebum
thickhead
waste man